100 GREATS

SOUTHEND UNITED FOOTBALL CLUB

100 GREATS
GREATS

SOUTHEND UNITED FOOTBALL CLUB

WRITTEN BY
DAVE GOODY & PETER MILES

TEMPUS

First published 2001
Copyright © Dave Goody and Peter Miles, 2001

Tempus Publishing Limited
The Mill, Brimscombe Port,
Stroud, Gloucestershire, GL5 2QG

ISBN 0 7524 2177 8

Typesetting and origination by
Tempus Publishing Limited
Printed in Great Britain by
Midway Colour Print, Wiltshire

Present and forthcoming football titles from Tempus Publishing:

Another Day at the Office (Roger Freestone)	Pb 128pp	Keith Haynes	0 7524 2167 9	£12.99
Cambridge United FC	Images	Attmore & Nurse	0 7524 2256 1	£9.99
Charlton Athletic FC	Images	David Ramzan	0 7524 1504 2	£9.99
Coventry City FC	Greats	George Rowland	0 7524 2294 4	£9.99
Crystal Palace FC	Greats	Revd Nigel Sands	0 7524 2176 X	£12.00
Everton FC 1880-1946	Images	John Rowlands	0 7524 2259 6	£10.99
Forever England	Pb 192pp	Mark Shaoul	0 7524 2042 9	£17.99
Gillingham FC	Images	Roger Triggs	0 7524 1567 0	£9.99
Gillingham FC	Players	Roger Triggs	0 7524 2243 X	£17.99
Ipswich Town FC	Images	Tony Garnett	0 7524 2152 2	£9.99
Leeds United FC	Images	David Saffer	0 7524 1642 1	£9.99
Leeds United in Europe	Images	David Saffer	0 7524 2043 7	£9.99
Leyton Orient FC	Images	Neilson Kaufman	0 7524 2094 1	£10.99
Manchester City FC	Classics	David Saffer	0 7524 2255 3	£12.00
Millwall FC 1885-1939	Images	Millwall FC Museum	0 7524 1849 1	£9.99
Queens Park Rangers FC	Images	Tony Williamson	0 7524 1604 9	£9.99
Reading FC	Greats	David Downs	0 7524 2081 X	£9.99
Reading FC 1871-1997	Images	David Downs	0 7524 1061 X	£9.99
Sniffer (Allan Clarke)	Hb 192pp	David Saffer	0 7524 2168 9	£17.99
Southend United FC	Images	Miles & Goody	0 7524 2089 5	£9.99
Voices of '66	Images	Norman Shiel	0 7524 2045 3	£9.99

Introduction

In Eduardo Galeano's excellent book on South American soccer, *Football in Sunshine and Shadow*, he offers the following confession. 'Like all children, I wanted to be a professional footballer. I played quite well, in fact I was terrific, but only at night when I was asleep.' How many of you are in the same boat as him? When you finally realise that you are never going to be good enough to play for your favourite team, the next best thing is to be a supporter. The faces around you become familiar, lasting friendships are made, and you claim your position in the ground. You belong and you share the same dreams as the people each side of you. The players that wear your club's shirt become your idols and you want to be them.

Over 900 players have played for Southend United since their formation in 1906, some great and many distinctly less so. The title of this book is *100 Greats*, although we would not be churlish enough to suggest that it is a definitive list of the 'greatest' players, as many of them played long before either of us were born. The selection has been our personal choice, comprising our own favourites and players that we never saw play but have come to appreciate as club folklore and history is passed down from older and wiser heads. We hope you enjoy our selection of players and their career retrospectives; I know our schoolboy heroes are in here, we hope yours are too.

Peter Miles
Southend-on-Sea
August 2001

ABOUT THE AUTHORS

Dave Goody was born in Rochford and was destined to be a Southend United supporter from an early age, being the son of a longstanding Blues fan. Always a keen collector of statistics, he began collating information on the club which would turn into a ten-year journey before every result, goalscorer and line-up in the club's history had been located and logged. His marathon trek culminated in the publication of the seminal work *Southend United – The Official History* (Yore Publications 1993), which he co-wrote with Peter Mason. This is his fourth book on The Blues having co-written *Potted Shrimps* (Yore 1999) and *Images of Sport – Southend United Football Club* (Tempus 2000) with Peter Miles. He has amassed one of the biggest known collections of Southend United programmes and memorabilia. He lives in Hockley, is married to Karen and has a young son, Matthew.

Having been fortunate to be whisked away from the bowels of Arsenal territory as a small child, Peter Miles embarked on his love affair with the Shrimpers in 1976 and has been a regular at home and away games for a quarter of a century. He is a supreme optimist, with every new season 'going to be our season' no matter how bad things look. This is his sixth published football work and his third collaboration with Dave Goody. A self confessed stadium addict, he has photographed thousands of stadia all around the world and is also a regular contributor to *Groundtastic*, the respected football grounds magazine. He lives a stone's throw from his spiritual home and is married to Cathy.

STATISTICAL NOTE

The statistics boxes on certain players show the details of their first spells at the club, players marked with an asterisk subsequently rejoined the club.

ACKNOWLEDGEMENTS

We would like to acknowledge the continued co-operation of Southend United Football Club and also thank Associated Sports Photography for permission to use some of the photographs in this volume. Special thanks go to the family of Billy Moore: Janet and Charles Moore and Nicola Moore-Eltringham. Once again we appreciate the efforts of James Howarth and his staff at Tempus for bringing this project to fruition.

We would also like to thank Alan Bushell for the use of some photos in this and previous books. Every effort has been made to ensure that copyright has not been infringed, and apologies are offered should any such infringements have inadvertently occurred.

100 SOUTHEND GREATS

Sandy Anderson
Brett Angell
Fred Baron
Kevin Baron
Micky Beesley
Ian Benjamin
Tony Bentley
Billy Best
Stuart Brace
Peter Butler
Richard Cadette
Mervyn Cawston
Phil Chisnall
Paul Clark
Stan Collymore
Lou Costello
David Crown
Dave Cusack
Reg Davies
Tommy Dixon
Dickie Donoven
Frank Dudley
Dave Elliott
Jimmy Evans
Eddie Firmani
Andy Ford
Neil Freeman
John 'Jackie' French
Bill Garner
Bobby Gilfillan
Billy Goodwin
Cyril Grant
Terry Gray
Chris Guthrie
Tony Hadley
Harold Halse
Ian 'Chico' Hamilton

Ted 'Gunner' Hankey
Billy Hick
Roy Hollis
David Jack
Bob Jackson
Peter Johnson
Terry Johnson
Emlyn 'Mickey' Jones
Bobby Kellard
Harry Lane
Mike Lapper
Micky Laverick
Jimmy Lawler
Mike Marsh
Dave Martin
Jimmy McAlinden
Sammy McCrory
Roy McDonough
John McGuigan
John McKinven
Keith Mercer
George Molyneux
Stan Montgomery
Alan Moody
Billy Moore
Gary Moore
Colin Morris
Garry Nelson
Ricky Otto
Anton Otulakowski
Derrick Parker
Glenn Pennyfather
Steve Phillips
Ronnie Pountney
Chris Powell
Trevor Roberts
Dave Robinson

Arthur Rowley
Paul Sansome
Jimmy Shankly
Frank Sheard
Albert 'Joe' Sibley
Peter Silvester
Andy Smillie
Alf Smirk
Dave Smith
Ray J. Smith
Derek Spence
Micky Stead
Jim Stirling
Les Stubbs
Peter Taylor
Cyril Thompson
Harry Threadgold
Steve Tilson
Neil Townsend
Albert Wakefield
Frank Walton
Peter Watson
Dave Webb
Ronnie Whelan
Arthur Williamson
Steve Yates

The top 20, who appear here in italics, occupy two pages instead of the usual one.

Sandy Anderson
Defender

Born: Auchtermuchty, Fife, 20/2/1930
Joined: April 1950, from Newburgh Juniors
First team debut: v. Ipswich, 9/9/50
Appearances: 483
Goals: 8
Other clubs: Newburgh, 1947-50; Folkestone, 1963-65

Alexander 'Sandy' Anderson was born in the small Fife village of Auchtermuchty and started his fledgling football career on the banks of the Firth of Tay with nearby junior outfit Newburgh. He cut an impressive figure, being lithe and athletic with a shock of red hair. Even though the war was mercifully over, National Service was still compulsory and Anderson was stationed at Shoebury Garrison, where he was a physical training instructor.

In April 1950, Southend manager Harry Warren happened, quite by chance, to be at the garrison for a match in which Anderson was playing. Warren immediately offered him a contract, although both men would have to wait until Anderson demobilised on completion of his National Service the following September. He took over from Frank Walton at left-back on a regular basis in December and made the position his own for the next thirteen seasons. He scored his first goal for the club against Nottingham Forest in April 1951 and also became an occasional penalty taker. Later that month, Anderson missed two spot kicks in one match as The Blues had to settle for a 1-1 draw at home to Port Vale.

Anderson was ever present during the 1951/52 season and gained acclaim on one of The Blues' many pre-season European tours. Southend had beaten German side Worms

6-5 with the Scotsman scoring two unstoppable free kicks. The influential German football magazine Der Kicker reviewed Southend's progress in remaining matches against Mannheim and Saarbrucken and eulogised Anderson's forceful play. Anderson suffered a rare injury during 1952/53 when he sustained knee damage in a 4-2 defeat at Torquay in November which sidelined him for the remainder of the campaign. During 1955/56 he again had an injury-plagued season which would see him playing only nine games. The worst setback came in a match against Watford at Roots Hall in April 1956, which would see him out of the side until November.

He restored his full-back partnership with the equally consistent Scotsman Arthur Williamson during 1957/58, a season which saw Anderson selected by the Football Association for a representative match against Cambridge University. In May 1957, at the veteran age of twenty-seven, Anderson's consistency and loyalty was rewarded by the club when he was named co-beneficiary with Jimmy Stirling in a testimonial match against a Select XI. In October 1959, his selection for the match at Port Vale saw Anderson exceed Dickie Donoven's longstanding League appearance record when Anderson played his 319th Football League game in a Blues shirt. At the end of that season he was again

ALEX ANDERSON
Southend United

named co-beneficiary when, along with fellow stalwarts Arthur Williamson and Sam McCrory, he was awarded the proceeds from games against West Ham and Newcastle at Roots Hall.

Anderson was again a virtual ever-present for the next two seasons, but eventually lost his place in the team in November 1962, when Ted Fenton signed the stylish John Neal from Aston Villa. Anderson announced his retirement from the full-time game in the summer of 1963. He wound down his playing career with a couple of seasons at Folkestone Town. In forty years, only Alan Moody has ever tested Anderson's club record of 452 League appearances and in the modern day professional football culture of Bosman free transfers and money-grabbing agents, a one-club career is very much a thing of the past. Sandy Anderson's well-earned place in the club's long history, however, will never be forgotten.

Brett Angell
Striker

Born: Marlborough, Devon, 20/8/1968

Joined: July 1990, from Stockport

First team debut: v. Huddersfield, 25/8/90

Appearances: 128(8)

Goals: 63

Other clubs: Portsmouth, 1986-87; Cheltenham, 1987-88; Derby, 1987-88; Stockport, 1988-90 & 1996-2001; Everton, 1993-95; Sunderland, 1995-97; Walsall, 2000-01

Southend United supporters had been spoilt for prolific goalscorers during the 1980s, with the likes of Steve Phillips, Richard Cadette and David Crown attaining legendary status at Roots Hall. When the lattermost was somewhat surprisingly sold to Gillingham in the summer of 1990, Blues fans needed a new hero and Brett Angell fitted the bill perfectly.

Angell's career had started as a trainee with Portsmouth but the then Pompey manager, Alan Ball, decided the young striker would not make the grade and released him in the summer of 1987. Angell then had spells with non-League side Cheltenham Town, Derby County, and Stockport County, before moving to Southend. A tribunal fixed fee of £100,000 brought Angell to Roots Hall and he made an immediate impact, scoring on his debut in a 2-1 victory at Huddersfield.

Angell formed a brilliant three-man strike force, with Andy Ansah and Ian Benjamin, as Southend stormed to a second straight promotion and elevation to the Second Division for the first time in the club's history. Angell top scored with 26 League and cup goals – which included four in a remarkable 10-1 Leyland DAF Cup success over Aldershot. The 1991/92 campaign saw Angell finish the season with 23 goals.

The 1992/93 season was ruined by a serious injury when, in the pre-season period, it was dis-covered that Angell had a blood clot in his thigh which required complicated surgery. He did not regain his place in the team until February, by which time Stan Collymore had well and truly taken over as the Roots Hall goalscoring idol.

The 1993/94 season saw new signings Jason Lee and Tommy Mooney offer stiff competition to Angell – who angered Fry and Blues fans by publicly hinting at his desire to leave the club. He left for less-than-successful spells with Everton and Sunderland, returning to Stockport in the summer of 1996. He then top scored with 20 as County gained promotion to Division One.

The 1997/98 season saw Angell in prolific form, hitting 23 goals for Stockport as they consolidated their position in Division One. He top scored again in the following campaign and his goals were a vital factor in County's successful avoidance of relegation. However, the 1999/2000 season saw Angell in dispute with County's new manager, Andy Kilner, and he was transfer-listed, finally leaving the club for Walsall. Brett Angell has proved to be one of the most prolific Football League goalscorers of the last decade and, despite awkward style and a lack of pace, possesses the priceless knack of arriving in the right place at the right time. His deadly accuracy at Roots Hall was a pivotal feature of The Blues rise to unprecedented heights in the early 1990s.

Fred Baron

Striker

Born: Prudhoe, Northumberland, 29/12/1901

Died: 1996

Joined: March 1927, from Liverpool

First team debut: v. Newport, 12/3/27

Appearances: 64

Goals: 42

Other clubs: Mid-Rhondda, 1922-24; Liverpool, 1924-27

If you were asked which Southend United player has the greatest ratio of goals per game you would probably answer Hollis, Shankly, Best, Crown or Cadette – chances are you would not mention the name of Fred Baron. However, the diminutive forward from Prudhoe holds that record, with a fantastic return of 42 goals in 62 League matches. Strangely, as a youngster Baron was overlooked by several clubs in the North East, who all considered him too slight to make the grade in the professional game. He rose to prominence with Mid-Rhondda, between stints in the professional Southern League during the early 1920s.

He scored freely at that level for two seasons and came to the attention of the Liverpool manager, Matt McQueen, who signed him during the summer of 1924. He spent three seasons at Anfield, but could not really establish a regular place in the side. In his first season he scored 5 goals in only 9 appearances and followed with 2 in 10 starts in the 1925/26 season.

The 1926/27 campaign saw Baron figure only once in Liverpool's first eleven and when Ted Birnie enquired about his availability he found that he was able to bring the little striker to The Kursaal in March 1927. Baron made his Blues debut later that month in place of the injured Billy Goodwin. His small frame often saw him suffer the brunt of crude challenges and, sadly, Baron was seriously injured in the final game of that season at Bournemouth, which would sideline him for sometime. Baron regained his place in the side in late February and finished the campaign with the remarkable record of 12 goals from 12 matches.

The 1928/29 season was again ravaged by injury as Baron fractured a leg at Newport in December. The 1929/30 season gave Baron the chance to shine as, despite figuring in only 25 League matches, he top scored with an incredible 22 goals, including a hat-trick in a 6-0 demolition of Bristol Rovers. However, in the last game of the season, Baron suffered another broken leg.

He regained fitness for the 1931/32 season, contributing 5 goals as Southend finished in their highest League position at that time of third in the Third Division (South). Baron suffered yet another injury at Bristol Rovers in April 1932 and, despite being only thirty years old, he announced his retirement from the game at the end of that campaign. Sadly, he died in 1996, aged ninety-five, and it was a time for reflecting on what he might have achieved but for his desperately bad luck with injuries.

Kevin Baron
Striker

Born: Preston, Lancashire, 19/7/1926

Died: 1971

Joined: May 1954, from Liverpool

First team debut: v. Shrewsbury, 21/8/54

Appearances: 150

Goals: 46

Other clubs: Preston North End, 1945-46; Liverpool, 1946-53; Northampton, 1958-59; Gravesend, 1959-60; Aldershot, 1960-61

The youngest of nine brothers, Kevin was the only one of them to progress to play League football, with a career that took in spells at four different clubs. Kevin turned professional with Liverpool in August 1946, after beginning his career as an amateur with Preston North End. After making his debut in the 1947/48 season, Kevin played 140 times in the League for The Reds, scoring 32 goals and making an appearance in the 1950 FA Cup final against Arsenal. Baron had to settle for a runners-up medal, however, as Liverpool lost 2-0 in front of 100,000 spectators at Wembley. He transferred to Southend United in May 1954 after Harry Warren saw him as a good foil for the prolific Roy Hollis, who had recently been signed from Tottenham. The pair immediately formed a formidable partnership: Baron scored 18 goals in his first season with The Blues from his inside-left position, Hollis rattled in 32. Kevin got his only hat-trick for Southend in a 4-1 Christmas Day victory over Norwich City at The Stadium.

After playing in both the final game at The Stadium and the first game at Roots Hall, Kevin's 1955/56 season was truncated by a broken leg, sustained at Coventry in March 1956. The injury was so severe that he did not return to the first team for eleven months, marking the occasion in January 1957 by opening the scoring in a 2-0 defeat of Exeter City. He finished that season in style, scoring in four of the final six matches of the campaign.

After scoring 5 goals in 48 League and cup games during the 1957/58 season, Kevin left The Blues in September 1958 to join Northampton Town. Although he had a fairly successful season, his best days were behind him, and he drifted out of the professional game to join Gravesend & Northfleet. Baron scored on his debut in a 2-0 victory over Yeovil Town with another former Southend player, Jackie Bridge, also on the scoresheet. There were other familiar faces at his new club, Peter Heathcote and Crichton Lockhart also being in the team.

After a season in non-League football, Baron was bought back into the professional game by Aldershot in July 1960. Six appearances that season brought to an end a Football League career which had seen him score 81 goals in 309 League appearances – 45 of those goals being scored for The Blues. Kevin Baron was only forty-five when he died in 1971. Sadly, the Baron family were brought back into the news in April 1989, eighteen years after Kevin's death, when his brother, Gerard, became the oldest victim of the Hillsborough stadium disaster.

Micky Beesley
Striker

Born: High Beach, Essex, 10/6/1942

Joined: August 1962, from West Ham*

First team debut: v. Watford, 18/8/62

Appearances: 221(18)

Goals: 49

Other clubs: West Ham, 1959-62; Peterborough, 1965-67

Born near Epping Forest, Micky Beesley was always likely to sign for West Ham United. During his formative years at South West Ham Technical College, Beesley played alongside the likes of Alan Mullery, Geoff Hurst, Terry Venables and Ron Harris for West Ham, London and Essex schoolboys. Beesley joined West Ham as an apprentice professional straight from school, although his first-team chances would be limited during his three-year stay at Upton Park.

In August 1962, Ted Fenton, who had been Hammers manager for eleven years until 1961, persuaded him to join The Blues in a double-deal with Derek Woodley. Beesley's Southend career got off to a spectacular start when he scored eight goals in his first five outings, which included a hat-trick in a dramatic 4-3 triumph at Highfield Road against Coventry City. However, with Jim Fryatt returning from injury, the latter part of the campaign saw Beesley struggling to hold a place in the side. By the end of the season, Beesley had a more-than-respectable return of 16 goals from 29 games.

The 1963/64 season saw Beesley lead the way with 13 goals – one ahead of youngster Ray Smith. The signings of Bobby Gilfillan and Jimmy Conway provided even stiffer competition for the forward positions. The 1964/65 season, Fenton's last in charge of The Blues, saw Beesley in and out of the side. Beesley totalled 34 goals in 79 appearances before, surprisingly, moving to Peterborough United in July 1965. His departure coincided with Alvan Williams' arrival as manager. In an attempt to make a big impact, Williams splashed out a club record £10,000 on bringing former Italian international, Eddie Firmani, to the club. Beesley's two-year stint at London Road was much less successful, and he returned to Roots Hall in the summer of 1967. Southend were now under the guidance of Ernie Shepherd, and Beesley would prove a useful and versatile member of his squad, not only playing up front but also performing strongly in defence and working tirelessly in midfield. In his second spell at the club, he passed the 200-appearance mark and took his tally of goals to 49. In the summer of 1971, despite still only being twenty-nine, Beesley was released by Arthur Rowley and joined Southern League Dover. Although known as a utility player, Micky never suffered from the 'jack of all trades, master of none' syndrome which often afflicts players who can perform in many different positions – he was good enough in any role to retain his place in the first team.

Ian Benjamin
Striker

Born: Nottingham, 11/12/1961

Joined: March 1990, from Exeter

First team debut: v. Carlisle, 3/3/90

Appearances: 139

Goals: 37

Other clubs: Sheffield Utd, 1978-79; West Brom, 1979-81; Notts County, 1981-82; Peterborough, 1982-84; Northampton, 1984-87; Cambridge, 1987-88; Chester, 1988-89; Exeter, 1989-90; Luton, 1992-93; Brentford, 1993-94; Wigan Athletic, 1994-95

Nottingham-born Ian experienced a baptism of fire in his League debut for Sheffield United in May 1979. The seventeen-year-old England youth international started for the first time in the final game of the 1978/79 season; a game that Sheffield United had to win to stand any chance of avoiding relegation to the Third Division. The gangly striker duly showed his mettle by converting two penalties in the 2-2 draw with Leicester City. Unfortunately, with Charlton Athletic winning, The Blades were still relegated, but this game showed the nerveless character that would serve Ian well during his fifteen-year career.

From Sheffield United, Ian moved on to West Bromwich Albion and then Notts County before a move to Peterborough United in August 1982 kick-started his career. He was an ever-present during his time there, but he was given a free transfer, and moved to Northampton, where he top scored in two consecutive seasons. Northampton won the Fourth Division title in 1986/87 – a season which also saw Southend promoted – and Ian notched 18 goals as an ever-present in the side.

In 1987/88, Ian left Northampton Town for brief spells at Cambridge United, Chester City, and Exeter City, before signing for Southend in March 1990. Renewing his partnership with David Crown, Ian helped The Blues to promo-tion from the Fourth Division, before partnering Brett Angell in the unforgettable 1990/91 season, which saw The Blues rise to the Second Division for the first time, and Ian score the most famous goal in the club's history – the strike at Bury that secured promotion through a 1-0 victory. The 1991/92 Second Division campaign again saw Brett and Ian top the scoring charts for The Blues, as they finished a more-than-respectable twelfth. The following season saw things turn sour for Ian, and after 7 goals in 16 League appearances, he left for Luton Town, to be replaced by Stan Collymore.

Ian's career after The Blues never hit the heights again, and after brief spells with Luton, Brentford and Wigan Athletic, he retired from the professional game with 486 League appearances and 126 goals to his name. He later played and managed extensively on the non-League circuit. Described as a 'model professional' by manager David Webb, Ian will always be remembered as the man who scored the goal that took The Blues to previously unseen heights; his return as a part-time 'goalscoring coach' during the 2000/01 season brought back great memories for many Blues fans.

Tony Bentley
Midfielder

Born: Stoke-on-Trent, Staffordshire, 20/12/1939

Joined: May 1961, from Stoke

First team debut: v. Bradford, 19/8/61

Appearances: 417(2)

Goals: 17

Other clubs: Stoke, 1956-61

Stoke-born Tony signed for his local club as a winger upon leaving school in 1956. After managing 15 goals in 44 appearances, Tony found that a regular first-team place with the Potters was beyond him, and moved south to join The Blues in May 1961. Serving under six different managers at Southend, Tony began his Blues career in a wide, attacking role, but, under the guidance of Ted Fenton, switched to the right-half berth in 1962/63. The following season saw Tony continue in his midfield role (although a lack of goals saw him tried at centre forward for a few games), and his 100 per cent endeavour earned him respect and even adulation from the Roots Hall fans.

At the end of the 1964/65 season, new Blues manager Alvan Williams moved Tony to right-back, a position which he went on to make his own. Bentley was voted Southend United's inaugural Player of the Year at the end of the 1965/66 season. In May 1966 he was also awarded a benefit match against a star-studded Stoke City side. Although the 1965/66 campaign would end in disappointment, as the Blues were relegated for the first time since joining the Football League, the

summer of 1967 saw new manager Ernie Shepherd appoint Tony club captain – a task he undertook with relish. Unfortunately, he was forced to miss quite a few games during the 1968/69 season after a cartilage operation, the Blues' campaign seeming to lose its focus during his absence. A mystery injury sustained at Bradford City in the League Cup in November 1969 proved to be even more serious than the cartilage problem, and he played no more part in the 1969/70 season.

A back operation to remove a troublesome disc led to many people writing off Tony's comeback chances, but Arthur Rowley reappointed him as club captain for the 1970/71 season, which was to prove the last in League soccer for Tony. The two major injuries had taken their toll, and although he was offered a chance to continue in League football with Port Vale, a move back to the Potteries did not appeal to Tony and his wife, who were both settled in the Southend area. Unusually, he was awarded a second testimonial match against his only other League club, Stoke City, in May 1972, when a crowd of 11,463 turned up to pay tribute to a great servant and wonderful captain.

Tony then joined Folkestone Town, newly promoted to the Premier Division of the Southern League, allowing him to continue

teaching and coaching the youngsters at various youth clubs and schools in the town. He later played for Ashford Town in the Southern League before emigrating to Canada in 1974. He currently lives in Kentville, Nova Scotia, and works as an events manager for Kentville Parks and Leisure. He returned to England in November 1999, to celebrate his sixtieth birthday with his UK-based relatives. Bentley also took time to visit his former mentor, Ernie Shepherd, at his home in Eastwood. Certainly, Bentley would have felt the loss of the former Southend manager keenly, following Shepherd's death, aged eighty-one, in March 2001.

Billy Best
Striker

Born: Glasgow, Scotland, 7/9/1943

Joined: January 1968, from Northampton

First team debut: v. Chester, 27/1/68

Appearances: 246(1)

Goals: 123

Other clubs: Pollock, 1960-62; Northampton, 1962-67 & 1973-77

In five seasons at Roots Hall, Billy Best secured a lasting place in the folklore of Southend United. Best is second only to Roy Hollis as the most prolific goalscorer in the club's history. What makes Best's achievement all the more remarkable is that it happened when The Blues were a struggling side and when football had abandoned the free-flowing playing style of the 1950s in favour of the more defensive formation of 4-4-2.

Billy Best was born in Mount Ellen in Glasgow and began his football career with a local junior outfit, Lochend Rovers. He then moved into adult football with a well-known Glaswegian amateur club, Pollock. At the age of eighteen, he was offered a contract by Northampton Town manager Dave Bowen in September 1962. True to form, Best scored on his League debut against Norwich City, despite being played as a winger. During his first spell with The Cobblers, Best and his team-mates enjoyed a truly amazing period as they were promoted from the Third Division to the First before sinking back down to the Fourth by the end of the decade. Best, however, left the County Ground for The Blues in January 1968

and would prove to be the greatest of Ernie Shepherd's many astute signings for the club. He quickly made his mark at Southend, scoring the first of a club record 9 hat-tricks against Chester in March 1968 and finished that season with 14 goals – only three adrift of top scorer Phil Chisnall, who had played more than twice as many games.

Despite figuring in just 20 games in the 1967/68 season, the newcomer was voted Player of the Year by Southend supporters. In the 1968/69 season, Best top scored with 31 goals – including an astonishing 10 in only four FA Cup ties. In the first round against Kings Lynn he scored three in a 9-0 victory, but in the next round Brentwood were annihilated 10-1, Best scoring five times with four coming in the last six minutes of the game. Best would retain his leading scorer's crown with 24 goals in the 1969/70 season. His most remarkable performance of that campaign came at Peterborough United in March 1970, when he hit a hat-trick between the 13th and 18th minute of the first half, before striking a fourth goal to secure a dramatic 4-3 triumph. In a season of struggle for The Blues, the club finished seventeenth in the Fourth Division. Best was the shining light and became the first Southend footballer to win the Player of the Year award for a second time.

Billy Best receives his second Player of the Year award from chairman Bill Rubin.

Southend fared even worse in 1970/71 under Arthur Rowley, but Best was leading scorer for a third successive season. In 1971/72 he lost that cherished title, finishing six goals behind Bill Garner, but adding two more hat-tricks – against Grimsby in September and Reading in March – to surpass Roy Hollis and Jimmy Shankly's jointly held club record of 7 hat-tricks. The season ended in style for The Blues as the club finally regained their place in the Third Division.

In his final season at Roots Hall, Rowley played Best in a supporting role to the two main strikers, Chris Guthrie and Gary Moore, and consequently Best had a relatively low return of 12 goals. In the summer of 1973, Rowley, somewhat surprisingly, allowed Best to rejoin Northampton – thus leaving him twelve goals short of the club record of 135 held by Roy Hollis. He spent another four seasons with The Cobblers, which included a couple of campaigns playing alongside a future Blues goalscoring legend, Steve Phillips.

At the end of the 1974/75 season, Best took the Northampton Player of the Year award. In keeping with his first spell at the County Ground, Best's goalscoring ratio dramatically declined, although in his later years he played in midfield. Best was released at the end of the 1977/78 season, when he joined Southern League Bedford Town. Billy Best was a schoolboy hero to a generation of young Southend supporters, and his goalscoring prowess has yet to be replicated – although many have made notable efforts. It is a lasting shame that he was not allowed another season to try and overhaul Roy Hollis' club record. In the modern era of decreasing club loyalty, the feats of Best and Hollis are now unlikely ever to be challenged. Billy Best currently lives and works in Bedford.

Stuart Brace
Striker

Born: Taunton, Somerset, 21/9/1942

Joined: October 1973, from Grimsby

First team debut: v. Hereford, 13/10/73

Appearances: 122(6)

Goals: 43

Other clubs: Taunton, 1959-60; Plymouth Argyle, 1960-65; Watford, 1965; Mansfield, 1965-67; Peterborough, 1967-68; Grimsby, 1968-73

Taunton-born Stuart Brace first came to the notice of the Football League club scouts when he scored seven times in a county youth game for Somerset. They won 10-2 and Exeter City, Torquay United and Bristol City were all interested in the diminutive striker, who was to go on to score over 150 goals in just over 400 League appearances for six different clubs. His playing career started with non-league Taunton Town but, after an unsuccessful trial with First Division Birmingham City, he signed, in November 1960, for Second Division Plymouth Argyle. He spent nearly five years with the Devon club, but only managed 9 appearances, without scoring, in the first team.

In September 1965, Stuart moved east, joining Watford, where he made 16 appearances and scored 4 goals in the 1965/66 season. A move north, to Mansfield Town, followed, and Stuart bagged 25 goals in a little over 50 League appearances. He then spent time with Peterborough United and Grimsby Town, where he really settled into the scoring groove, becoming known as a real 'goalpoacher' and when it became known that Stuart was

unhappy at Blundell Park, after five years, there were many clubs after his signature.

Stuart signed for Southend for a fee of £6,000 in October 1973 and certainly enjoyed his stay at Roots Hall, scoring on his debut in a 2-1 home victory over Hereford United in October 1973. He followed this with two goals in his second game, and then a hat-trick in his fourth appearance (a 5-2 home win over Huddersfield Town) – which meant that he had scored six goals in his first four games for the club. He finished the season with 22 goals in 38 appearances, and followed this feat with 12 in 52 games in the 1974/75 season.

The 1975/76 season saw Stuart drifting in and out of the team, having to share the striking duties with Peter Silvester and Stuart Parker. A diminished return of 9 goals in 38 appearances, including both goals in a 2-0 Boxing Day win at home to Colchester United, proved to be the end of the road in Stuart's League football career, and in July 1976 he left Southend and Roots Hall to return to his native West Country with Falmouth Town, who were playing in the Western League. Like his father before him, who had been a professional player with Bristol City, Stuart made himself an invaluable player with a lot of effort and an uncanny knack of knowing where the net was.

Peter Butler
Midfielder

Born: 27/8/1966

Joined: February 1988, from Cambridge

First team debut: v. Bristol Rovers, 13/2/88

Appearances: 160(7)

Goals: 12

Other clubs: Huddersfield, 1984-86; Bury, 1986; Cambridge, 1986-88; West Ham, 1992-94; Notts County, 1994-96; West Brom, 1995-98; Halifax, 1998-2000

When Dave Webb needed a rock in midfield to provide the backbone for Southend's surge up the divisions, he turned to Yorkshire-born Peter Butler, who was then with Cambridge United. Butler had started his playing career with brief spells at Huddersfield and Bury. He joined The Blues in February 1988 for a bargain fee of £45,000. Although Southend would suffer relegation to the Fourth Division on the last day of his first full season with the club, 1988/89, his hard work and ferocious tackling led to an immediate return the following campaign, when third place was secured. The adage that a club needs to 'kick' its way out of the basement division perhaps holds some truth when you look at Southend's midfield that season – Butler, Paul Clark and Dave Martin!

The 1990/91 season was an historic one for the club, as a second straight promotion was achieved, with Butler having a truly outstanding campaign. He missed only four games and was deservedly Player of the Year. It was a great shame that a brilliant season was not crowned with the Third Division championship, a last match defeat at home to Brentford allowing Cambridge to slip past and take the title by a single point. However, the 1991/92 season was a disaster for Butler as Southend enjoyed their first ever campaign in the Second Division. He suffered a variety of injuries and, when he did regain fitness, he found himself consigned to the substitutes bench as the central midfield berths had been taken by the experienced and stylish duo of Keith Jones and John Cornwell.

In March 1992, Butler spent a brief spell on loan to his first club, Huddersfield. However, it was no real surprise when West Ham signed him in the summer of 1992. In his first season with The Hammers, promotion to the Premiership was secured, and the following season, Butler was again a regular.

There then followed spells with Notts County (including a loan period with Grimsby) and West Brom. West Brom manager Alan Buckley saw Butler as his leader in midfield, but a serious injury and a hernia operation during his time there disrupted his run in the side and he was handed a free transfer by new manager Dennis Smith.

Butler returned to his hometown of Halifax as player-coach and then assistant manager to Mark Lillis, but in March 2000 his playing career was ended by a serious knee injury. Following a run of poor results, both Lillis and Butler were dismissed and Butler took a coaching job in Australia. In many ways, Peter Butler was the complete midfielder, being tenacious in the tackle but complementing that aggression with excellent distribution and the ability to create an opening for attacking players.

Richard Cadette
Striker

Born: Hammersmith, London, 21/3/1965

Joined: August 1985, from Leyton Orient

First team debut: v. Gillingham, 20/8/85

Appearances: 104(1)

Goals: 56

Other clubs: Wembley, 1982-84; Leyton Orient, 1984-85; Sheffield Utd, 1987-88; Brentford, 1988-92; Falkirk, 1992-94; Millwall, 1994-96

Although Richard Cadette possessed a frail-looking physique, his pace and ball control frightened the life out of lower division defences in the mid-1980s. As a teenager, Cadette came to prominence with Isthmian League outfit Wembley. After an impressive couple of seasons at Ive Farm, Cadette had made a successful adjustment from youth football and Orient manager Frank Clark had seen enough to offer the youngster a professional contract in August 1984.

The 1984/85 campaign was a disaster for The O's as they were relegated to the Fourth Division – with, incidentally, future Shrimper John Cornwell top scoring with 10 goals. Cadette played in around half the games, contributing 4 goals. In the summer of 1985, Cadette's team mate Barry Silkman had already signed for Southend and The Blues raided Brisbane Road again to snap up the young forward. The transfer was to be a protracted affair, with Clark wanting £10,000 for Cadette but Southend chairman Vic Jobson offering only £2,000. The dispute went to a Football League tribunal and the fee was fixed at £4,000. At the time, Jobson complained about the outcome but it was to prove an absolute steal.

Cadette made his first-team debut for Southend as a substitute in a Milk Cup tie at Gillingham in August 1985. His Football League debut came three days later, ironically against his old club, Orient. Cadette's performance was utterly unbelievable, his former colleagues being unable to contain him as his blistering pace saw him score four goals in a 5-1 demolition at Roots Hall. The remainder of that season saw Cadette hit a total of 25 goals, including another hat-trick in the home game with Rochdale. The following season, with Dave Webb in charge, saw Southend gain promotion to the Third Division. Cadette was even more prolific, scoring 31 League and cup goals, to become the first Blues player to top thirty goals in a campaign since Billy Best in 1968/69. Fittingly, Cadette was to score the decisive second goal in a 2-0 last game victory at Stockport, which saw The Blues secure the final promotion place ahead of Wolves.

Having topped a half-century of goals in only two seasons, Cadette was hot property and First Division Sheffield United won the race for his signature, with the fee again going to a tribunal. The sum of £130,000 was reached – once more leaving chairman Jobson seething, as 30 per cent of the money was to go to Orient as part of the original deal. Cadette spent an injury-plagued season at Bramall Lane and was offloaded to Brentford in the summer of 1988 for £80,000. Sadly,

injuries again affected his performances and he was unable to recapture his form in front of goal. He was briefly loaned to Bournemouth in March 1990 and was increasingly becoming a peripheral figure at Griffin Park under the management of Phil Holder. Yet another injury, sustained against West Brom in October 1991, saw him released from his contract at Brentford.

In January 1992, Falkirk manager, Jim Jefferies, offered him the chance to resurrect his career. He revived in the less taxing surroundings of Scottish Division One and top scored in his first full season – striking up a good partnership with veteran former Grimsby frontman Kevin Drinkell. The 1993/94 season at Brockville Park saw Cadette back to his prolific best, scoring 24 League and cup goals. This included one in the Scottish B&Q League Cup final, which saw The Bairns triumph 3-0 over St Mirren at Fir Park, Motherwell. The season was rounded off by claiming the Division One championship and, with it, promotion to the Premier League. Cadette started the new season in fine form, scoring both goals in a memorable 2-1 Scottish League Cup victory over a star-studded Rangers team at Ibrox.

Millwall manager Mick McCarthy parted with £135,000 in October 1994 to bring Cadette back to the Football League. His first season at The Den was ended in January 1995 with a knee ligament injury sustained against Oldham. A month earlier, Cadette had received a great ovation on his return to Roots Hall with The Lions, scoring the only goal in a 1-0 Millwall victory. He lost all the following campaign to injury except for one brief outing as a substitute late on in the season. The 1996/97 campaign was to be Cadette's last in the Football League. He managed only 7 games in yet another injury-blighted season and was given a free transfer by Lions boss Billy Bonds in the summer of 1997. He currently lives and owns a business in the Berkshire town of Slough.

Mervyn Cawston
Goalkeeper

Born: Diss, Norfolk, 4/2/1952

Joined: August 1974, from Norwich*

First team debut: v. Bury, 24/8/74

Appearances: 242

Goals: 0

Other clubs: Norwich, 1969-76; Chicago Sting (USA), 1975-78; Gillingham, 1976-77; Stoke, 1984-85

As a schoolboy in Norfolk, Mervyn was a talented athlete, winning the Norfolk schools pole vault championship before playing in goal for England schoolboys against West Germany. At fifteen years old, Cawston joined Norwich City, and soon established himself as understudy to the great Kevin Keelan. After limited appearances for The Canaries in the 1974/75 season, Norwich allowed Cawston to join Southend on loan. Unfortunately for Mervyn, Keelan suffered a rare injury, letting Roger Hansbury move past Cawston as second-choice custodian. After brief loan spells at Leicester City and Newport County, Cawston decided that he needed regular first-team football, so he left Carrow Road in May 1976 to join Gillingham. After a great start to his career at the Priestfield, in which The Gills went unbeaten for six games, things went wrong as the side lost six straight matches. Cawston took the brunt of the inevitable criticism and had his contract cancelled in April 1977.

At this point in his career, Cawston decided he needed a change, so he signed for North American Soccer League club, Chicago Sting and spent two seasons playing in the Atlantic Conference Northern Division. At the end of the second season, Blues' manager Dave Smith persuaded Mervyn that the time was right to return to England, and a fee of £20,000 secured his services. After making his second debut for Southend in the opening game of the 1978/79 season, he went from strength to strength, his agile shot stopping and domination of the penalty box making him one of Southend United's all-time greats. Although the club suffered relegation at the end of the 1979/80 season, the following campaign more than made up for it. Cawston was ever present in the side that broke so many club records, including: least home goals conceded (6), least total goals conceded (31), most clean sheets total (25), most home clean sheets (17) and most consecutive home clean sheets (10).

The 1981/82 season saw Cawston miss a lot of games through injury, and his absence coincided with a run of only 5 wins in 21 games. After two more seasons of irregular appearances, he finally left for Stoke in March 1984. However, he failed to break into the first team, and after a brief spell with Chelmsford City, he returned to Roots Hall in November 1984. After nine more matches for The Blues, he switched to the local non-League scene. Having grown to love the Southend area, Cawston has settled down there, and is now a successful financial advisor.

Phil Chisnall
Midfielder

Born: Manchester, 27/10/1942

Joined: August 1967, from Liverpool

First team debut: v. Port Vale, 19/8/67

Appearances: 156(5)

Goals: 32

Other clubs: Manchester Utd, 1959-63; Liverpool, 1964-67; Stockport, 1971-72

Phil was one of the original Busby Babes when he joined Manchester United from school at the age of fifteen in 1957. He had shone in representative matches for Stretford schools and already won England schoolboy caps against Scotland, Northern Ireland, Wales and Germany. It was a natural move for the Manchester-born lad, and he soon struck up a friendship with future Blues players Frank Haydock and Sammy McMillan. Originally he signed on at Old Trafford as an amateur, but when he was offered professional terms in November 1959, he was well on his way to realising his boyhood dream.

After some fleeting appearances in the star-studded first team he seemed to have finally made a breakthrough at the start of the 1963/64 season, when he played the first sixteen games of the campaign. However, despite some notable victories, Matt Busby was far from happy with his front line and signed Graham Moore from Chelsea in November 1963. Moore immediately took Chisnall's berth at inside right and, with the emergence of a young Ulsterman called George Best, Chisnall's future at Old Trafford was looking increasingly restricted.

After making 35 appearances in the famous red shirt and scoring 8 goals – while having been further honoured with England under-23 caps against Scotland, Wales, France and West Germany – Phil became one of the very few players to make the move across from Manchester to Liverpool in April 1964 for a fee of £25,000. After three seasons at Liverpool, in which he managed only 6 appearances and 1 goal, chairman Bill Rubin persuaded him to move south and join the Blues in a deal that cost the club £14,000. This meant that Phil was the costliest player ever purchased by Southend, until the signing of Bill Garner from Bedford Town in 1969.

Phil, whose Christian name is actually John, made a place in the Blues team his own and, during a four-year stay with the club, appeared in the first team over 150 times, his imposing midfield play being enjoyed by the Blues fans at a time when many 'greats' were in the Blues' first-team squad. In September 1971, Phil returned to the Manchester area, joining Stockport County, for whom he made 30 appearances in a disastrous campaign which saw County finish second bottom of the Fourth Divison, only three points ahead of Crewe Alexandra. At the end of that nightmare campaign, Chisnall was one of many Stockport players handed free transfers – including his former Blues team-mate Sammy McMillan. It was a real shame that Chisnall's League career ended at the relatively young age of thirty-one with the player never having truly realised his early potential.

Paul Clark
Midfielder

Born: Benfleet, Essex, 14/9/1958

Joined: July 1976, from apprentice*

First team debut: v. Brighton, 17/8/76

Appearances: 343(15)

Goals: 7

Other clubs: Brighton & Hove Albion, 1977-82; Gillingham, 1991-93; Chelmsford, 1993-95; Cambridge, 1995-96

Paul Clark was born in South Benfleet in September 1958, and played 8 times for England schoolboys before joining Southend United as an apprentice. After further representative honours for his country at youth level, Paul made his first-team debut for The Blues at the tender age of seventeen, coming on as a substitute against future employers Brighton in a League Cup tie at the Goldstone Ground in August 1975.

A man who would often play with his heart rather than his head, Paul quickly became a crowd favourite, with his rampaging runs and crunching tackles a prominent feature of any visit to Roots Hall when Paul was playing. After only 8 appearances in the 1977/78 season, Paul left the seaside of Southend for the seaside of Brighton, with Gerry Fell travelling in the opposite direction. Paul immediately fitted into The Seagulls midfield, playing alongside the likes of Brian Horton and Mark Lawrenson. Although still tender in years, Paul's style helped drive Brighton to the brink of the First Division, but with Tottenham gaining the point they needed in their final game, The Seagulls missed out on goal average.

The disappointment of 1977/78 did not hamper Brighton the following season, and again

they pressed for promotion to the top division under Alan Mullery. This time they were successful, finishing as runners-up to Crystal Palace, with Clark again pulling the strings in midfield. Unfortunately for Paul, the 1979/80 First Division campaign was blighted by injuries, and he played only 11 matches – although he did manage goals against Manchester City and Liverpool. Having clung onto their First Division status in 1979/80, The Seagulls did the same again the following season, but Paul played only a minor role, being unable to hold a place in the side on a regular basis.

The 1981/82 campaign was even worse, as Paul failed to make a single first-team appearance for Brighton. By the time the start of the 1982/83 campaign came around, Paul had left the South Coast for a return to his hometown club. The Blues were in the Third Division at the time, and Paul came back to the same adoring fans he had left. Although never managing to feature in the side for lengthy consecutive spells– his all-action style of play leading to several injuries and suspensions – Clark's influence on the team was huge, whether at centre half or in the heart of midfield.

After relegation at the end of the 1983/84 season, and the debacle of the following campaign, Paul's inspirational leadership began to take hold again, and after a ninth place finish

at the end of the 1985/86 season, The Blues appeared to be on a good thing with David Webb in charge and sitting in a promotion position with only three months of the 1986/87 season remaining.

However, Webb walked away from Roots Hall, and Paul was placed in charge of the team in a caretaker capacity. His on-the-field leadership was replicated off it, and an ever-present Clarky guided The Blues to promotion. He was disappointed not to be given the manager's job for the new season, but he did not have long to wait before the new incumbent, Dick Bate, was sacked. Only ten games of the 1987/88 season had elapsed when Clark received the call, and at twenty-nine years of age, became the youngest manager in the Football League. However, he found it more difficult the second time around and, after avoiding relegation only by winning the last three matches of the season, it was no surprise when Dave Webb

returned as general manager three months into the 1988/89 campaign.

This led to the eventual takeover of team affairs by Webb and once again Clark returned to his old rampaging self, but only on the field this time. After three more seasons as a player, and a testimonial match against Arsenal in February 1990, Clark was released from the club in July 1991. He joined Gillingham, where he featured as an ever-present during 1991/92, alongside former Shrimper, David Crown. The 1992/93 season saw Gillingham miss going out of the Football League by a narrow margin of four points and, after only thirteen games in the 1993/94 season, Clark hung up his boots. He then had a brief spell at Chelmsford City before linking up with ex-West Ham and Orient player, Tommy Taylor, as assistant manager at Cambridge United. In November 1996, both men moved to Leyton Orient – a post he held until November 2001.

Stan Collymore

Striker

Born: Stone, Staffordshire, 22/1/1971

Joined: November 1992, from Palace

First team debut: v. Notts County, 21/11/92

Appearances: 33

Goals: 18

Other clubs: Wolves, 1987-88; Stafford Rangers, 1990-91; Crystal Palace, 1991-92; Nottingham Forest, 1993-95; Liverpool, 1995-97; Aston Villa, 1997-99; Leicester, 1999-2000; Bradford, 2000-01; Real Oviedo (Spain), 2001

Stan Collymore was born in Stone, Staffordshire, and was an associate schoolboy with Wolves when he was dealt the first of many blows to his career. He was shown the door at Molineux and sought refuge with local Conference side, Stafford Rangers. He had a good start to the 1990/91 season and scored 12 goals in 23 games. His form was good enough to attract the attention of Steve Coppell, who signed him for Crystal Palace in January 1991 for £100,000. At Selhurst Park he was only an occasional player, making fleeting appearances as substitute. The youngster was in need of someone to believe in him and Colin Murphy was to be that man.

Murphy had taken over as manager of Southend United from the hugely popular Dave Webb at the start of the 1991/92 season, but by November Murphy was already the target of abuse from supporters as the side were struggling at the wrong end of the table. As part of their protests, fans boycotted the Notts County game, and a crowd of only 3,219 turned up to witness Collymore's debut. His terrific pace and direct style saw goals coming regularly and even set The Blues on a rare FA Cup run. However, despite his best efforts, Southend's League position was still perilous and a 4-0 defeat at Notts County and a 2-1 reversal at home to Tranmere Rovers spelt the end for Colin Murphy. He was

replaced by the irrepressible Barry Fry, who coaxed even more out of the young Midlander, Collymore's goals and a rejuvenated team spirit steering The Blues to safety. Fry later mentioned that Collymore had been a model professional and never missed training – despite constant round trips to his family home in Cannock to be at the bedside of his sister, who was tragically dying of cancer.

The celebration that came when relegation was staved off was tempered by the realisation that the club could not possibly hold onto its prize asset, but Barry Fry's well-earned reputation in the transfer market would soften the blow considerably. Stan Collymore was sold on to Nottingham Forest for an initial fee of £2.25 million and Fry's business acumen saw clauses negotiated in the deal that would bring increments to the transfer fee subject to appearances, goals, sell-on fees and international caps. At the City Ground, under the experienced coaching of Frank Clark, Collymore continued to improve. His two-season spell saw him score 45 times in only 78 matches. He was finally selected to play for England in the Umbro Cup matches against Japan and Brazil in the summer of 1995, just prior to his then British transfer record move to Liverpool for £8.5 million.

The huge sum that took him to Anfield saw the total fee Southend received for Collymore

rise to £3.57 million and, although £600,000 went to Crystal Palace in sell-on clauses, the club were able to finish the redevelopment of Roots Hall and purchase their own training ground complex. The gifted striker's indelible presence at Roots Hall was secured when the Stan Collymore Suite was opened in the East Stand. At Anfield, Collymore was often asked to play in an unfamiliar withdrawn role under Roy Evans. He still managed 35 goals in 81 games, but was largely considered a failure at the club.

In May 1997, The Reds were happy to recoup £7 million of their outlay by selling the striker to Aston Villa. Although goals were scarce, his form led to a recall to the national side as a substitute in a World Cup qualifier against Moldova. His Villa Park career turned sour, however, when Brian Little was sacked and replaced by John Gregory. Several Villa players, including Collymore, publicly criticised Gregory's man-management skills, and Collymore bore the brunt of his new manager's wrath. The tabloid media had long enjoyed Collymore's page-filling private life, but his heavily publicised break up with girlfriend Ulrika Jonsson in a Parisian restaurant spelt the end of his Villa career.

The 1998/99 season saw him loaned out to First Division Fulham. A brief and unsuccessful spell at Craven Cottage saw him return to Villa Park as an outcast, banished to training on his own or with the youth team. In February 1999, Leicester's Martin O'Neill paid £250,000 for Collymore. Despite media hype over another 'incident' – this time at Leicester's Spanish training camp retreat at La Manga – Collymore repayed O'Neill's faith with a stunning debut hat-trick against Sunderland. Tragically, after only six games, his season was ended with a broken leg. O'Neill's departure to Celtic saw Collymore at odds with new manager, Peter Taylor, who offloaded him to Bradford City.

Once again, Stan made an immediate impact, scoring a stunning overhead goal on his debut. However, yet again, Stan was to fall foul of a change of management that saw him become surplus to requirements. In January 2001, Collymore joined Real Oviedo. However, after only two appearances as substitute he was dropped from the squad due to a lack of fitness. In March 2001, he announced to a stunned football world that, at the age of thirty, he was retiring from the game to spend more time with his family. It is a shame that this gifted footballer will probably be remembered for his behaviour rather than his skill. It is, however, a credit to our little club that Stan acknowledges that he has only ever been truly happy at Roots Hall.

Lou Costello

Utility

Born: Barking, Essex, 8/7/1936

Joined: May 1957, from Aldershot

First team debut: v. Newport, 28/9/1957

Appearances: 266

Goals: 15

Other clubs: Leyton, 1953-56; Aldershot, 1956-67; Chelmsford, 1965-68

Mortimer 'Lou' Costello was born in July 1936 in Barking, and played for Athenian League Leyton before joining the Army. Costello was stationed at Aldershot and played for the local Third Division side. He spent one season with The Shots, 1956/57, and scored 7 times in 28 League outings. His job with the Army also meant he gained selection for the Army Amateur XI representative side.

Costello turned professional, signing for Southend in May 1957, and was taken on The Blues' pre-season tour to Austria and Czechoslovakia. He opened his Southend goal account by scoring a brace in a 4-0 defeat of Budjovice. He made his League debut for The Blues in a 1-0 defeat against Newport County in September 1957, and made a further eight appearances that season. Costello also played in the FA Cup matches against Trowbridge Town and Torquay United, but was replaced in the side by Jim Duthie for the third round tie with Liverpool that went to a replay, The Blues losing 3-2, having led at half-time.

The 1958/59 campaign saw Costello fully converted to the wing-half position and his 36 first-team appearances included the embarrass-

ing 1-0 FA Cup defeat to Yeovil Town. The 1959/60 season proved to be a more successful one for Costello, who contributed five goals. However, the following campaign was a poor one for both the club and Costello, as he only found the net once. During the 1961/62 season, The Blues were in the midst of a goal drought and Costello was pressed into service in his old centre forward position. However, he only managed to muster three successful strikes.

Costello's sterling service over five seasons was acknowledged with a benefit match against a star-studded Select XI in May 1962. Changing positions again, he made the right-back position his own during the 1962/63 campaign. In truth, The Blues had struggled to replace Arthur Williamson, and Costello was the most successful of the four players that had tried the troublesome position.

He was a regular for the next two seasons, but his appearance in the final game of the 1964/65 campaign was to be his last in a Blues shirt. The close season saw Ted Fenton replaced by Alvan Williams, who made several changes to the defence. With his new formation settled, Williams decided Costello was surplus to requirements. Costello had clocked up over 250 appearances in an eventful eight-season stint with The Blues, but in July 1965 he signed for Chelmsford City of the Southern League.

David Crown
Striker

Born: Enfield, Middlesex, 16/2/1958

Joined: November 1987, from Cambridge United

First team debut: v. Aldershot, 21/11/87

Appearances: 132

Goals: 69

Other clubs: Grays Athletic, 1977-78; Walthamstow Ave, 1978-80; Brentford, 1980-81; Portsmouth, 1981-83; Reading, 1983-85; Cambridge, 1985-87; Gillingham, 1990-92; Purfleet, 1992-96

David Crown was born in Enfield on 16 February 1958 and, as an eighteen-year-old, joined Grays Athletic. After two years he moved on to Walthamstow Avenue, where he attracted the attention of Brentford while playing as a left winger, and he signed for them in July 1980. After making a dream debut, scoring in a League Cup match against Charlton Athletic, David managed 46 League appearances and 6 goals before being transferred to Portsmouth in October 1981, in a deal that involved Chris Kamara travelling in the opposite direction.

Things didn't really work too well for David at Portsmouth, and following an indifferent run of form and a short loan spell at Exeter City, he dropped down a division to join Reading in August 1983. In his first season at Elm Park, David missed only one game and contributed 7 goals to a team that won promotion from the Fourth to the Third Division, with Trevor Senior banging in 36 League goals. In the following season – in which David scored another 7 goals and Reading held their own in the higher division – David became increasingly aware of the home crowd's hostility towards him. He was never able to work out why they took a dislike to him but, after an injury to Trevor Senior had meant that David moved from his left-wing position to a central

striking role, he scored two goals against Cambridge United – which impressed Cambridge's manager, Ken Shellito, enough to buy him.

David signed for Cambridge in July 1985, but the 1985/86 season was a bad one for United, who finished in the re-election zone in the Fourth Division. David still managed to rattle in 24 League goals, however, including nine in the final seven games of the campaign – amazingly, this still stands at the record number of goals in a season for a Cambridge United player. David scored 12 goals the following season, and after notching 9 goals in 17 League games at the start of the 1987/88 season, he joined Southend United in November, making his debut in a 0-0 home FA Cup match against Walsall. By the end of the season, David had scored 17 goals in only 28 League appearances for The Blues, and had the amazing record of being the season's top scorer for both Cambridge United and Southend United.

Already a hero at Roots Hall, David slammed home 29 goals in all competitions in the 1988/89 season, but unfortunately his

efforts were in vain as The Blues were relegated to the Fourth Division. Although he managed fewer goals the following season, 23 in 49 appearances, the support he received from others, such as Martin Ling (11 goals) and Gary Bennett (8 goals), meant the club gained promotion back to the Third Division under the guidance of David Webb. The final game of the season, in which Southend needed a win away at Peterborough United to secure the third promotion place, carved David's name into the folklore of the club, as he scored both goals in a famous 2-1 win.

Now aged thirty-two, David needed security for himself and his family. Having found the new contract on offer at Southend unsatisfactory, he moved across the Medway to Gillingham for the start of the 1990/91 season. Eleven goals in 30 injury-hit League appearances left Gillingham in mid-table in the Fourth Division. Although David managed a fine 22 goals in 36 appearances in 1991/92, Gillingham didn't manage a great deal, and David decided to go part-time – splitting his time between playing football in the non-League arena and working as an accountant. Spells with Dagenham, Purfleet, Aylesbury, Sudbury, Billericay and Concord Rangers ended with a final spell as player/assistant manager at Purfleet. Now working as an accountant and a summariser on Southend United matches on BBC Essex, David will always be remembered as one of the most deadly strikers to have worn the blue shirt of Southend.

Dave Cusack
Defender

Born: Thurcroft, South Yorkshire, 6/6/1956

Joined: September 1978, from Sheffield Wednesday

First team debut: v. Sheffield Wednesday, 9/9/78

Appearances: 212

Goals: 20

Other clubs: Sheffield Wed, 1974-78; Millwall, 1983-85; Doncaster Rovers, 1985-87; Rotherham, 1987-88; Boston, 1988-89; Doncaster Rovers, 1989-90

Dave made his debut for Sheffield Wednesday on 11 October 1975 and stayed in the team for the rest of the season, forming a formidable partnership with Scotsman Neil O' Donnell. However, after a mediocre 1976/77 season, Dave came into his own in the 1977/78 campaign, missing only three games before injury ended his season in March 1978. At the start of the 1978/79 campaign, Dave was approached about a transfer to Southend. Although he was unsure about leaving his beloved Sheffield, he signed in September 1978.

In no time at all, he formed an excellent partnership with Alan Moody. Having won the Southend supporters over with his skills and commitment at the heart of The Blues' defence, it was a disappointment for Dave when Southend were relegated at the end of the 1979/80 season. However, that was more than made up for when the team romped to the Fourth Division championship in the 1980/81 campaign, Dave being an integral part of the defence that set so many records that season. He also became a deadly penalty taker during the course of the campaign, smashing home four to add to the two goals he scored in open play.

Besides adding three more penalty conversions to his name in the 1981/82 season, Dave was beginning to make a name for himself as an impassable centre half, and his partnership with

Alan Moody would go down as one of the greatest in the history of Southend United Football Club. With the team sitting in the top ten of the Third Division at the end of March during the 1982/83 campaign, the Southend fans were outraged to hear that he was, along with Anton Otulakowski, being transferred to divisional rivals Millwall for a joint fee of £60,000. However, after Millwall won promotion to the Second Division at the end of the 1984/85 campaign, Dave was transferred to Third Division Doncaster Rovers before the start of the 1985/86 season. Having been signed by Billy Bremner, he subsequently took over the reins from him as player-manager during the 1986/87 campaign. Inauspiciously, he was sacked from this job, and not long afterwards from the same role at Rotherham. Dave then took over as manager of Boston United, before taking the reins at Kettering Town. He lost that job when the club went into receivership, and after a single non-contract appearance back at Doncaster Rovers in 1989, he returned south to manage Basildon United. In more recent years, he had a spell as chief executive of Scarborough, before once again becoming involved with Basildon United. After running a pub, Dave suffered horrific injuries in a car accident during 2000, which resulted in a broken neck. Thankfully, he is now well on the road to recovery.

Reg Davies

Striker

Born: Cymmer, Mid Glamorgan, 27/5/1929

Joined: July 1949, from Southampton

First team debut: v. Notts County, 17/12/49

Appearances: 42

Goals: 18

Other clubs: Southampton, 1947-49; Newcastle, 1951-58; Swansea, 1958-61; Carlisle, 1962-63

Reg signed as a professional at The Stadium in July 1949, and scored the opener on his first-team debut, on 17 December 1949, in the 2-0 home victory over Notts County. By the end of the season, he had made 14 appearances and scored 6 goals. Reg started the 1950/51 season as a first-team regular, and scored two goals in the opening game, a 5-1 home victory against Watford in front of 18,000 fans. By the time April 1951 came round, Reg had made 28 appearances and scored 12 goals – including a brace on five different occasions – and this form persuaded Newcastle United to splash out 'a large fee' (believed to be £10,000) for his services as an inside forward.

Reg made his debut for the mighty Magpies at the start of the 1951/52 campaign and, such was his rapid rise to fame, that by the start of the 1952/53 season he was already being spoken about as a Welsh international. The call didn't take long to come and, on 18 October 1952, Reg lined up for Wales against Scotland at Ninian Park, Cardiff – alongside such greats as Trevor Ford and Ivor Allchurch. Wales lost 1-2, but Reg played sufficiently well, with the great Charles Buchan of the *News Chronicle* reporting 'Davies

marked the ball cleverly and positioned intelligently in the first of what should be many games for Wales'. Reg was retained for the next game, at Wembley against England, but the 2-5 defeat saw Reg drop out of the international limelight for a while, although it didn't seem to affect his club form.

He was recalled to the Wales squad in October 1953, to partner John Charles and Ivor Allchurch, and played against England at Cardiff and Scotland at Hampden – where he helped the Welsh to a fine 3-3 draw. This time, however, he had to wait almost four years before his next call up, and he played against East Germany in a World Cup qualifier at Ninian Park on 25 September 1957, followed by a cap against England on 19 October 1957.

There were no more international call-ups and his spell at St James' Park ended in October 1958, after over 150 League appearances and 49 goals, when he joined Swansea City. He stayed with The Swans for nearly four years, before moving north to end his career with Carlisle United. Reg had recorded 109 League goals in 371 appearances when his career concluded after the 1963/64 season – an excellent record for a fine inside forward, who was one of the few to go on to international honours after starting their career with Southend United. Reg later managed non-League Kings Lynn.

Tommy Dixon
Midfielder

Born: Seaham Harbour, Co. Durham, 17/9/1899

Joined: June 1927, from Clapton Orient

First team debut: v. Luton, 27/8/27

Appearances: 265

Goals: 7

Other clubs: Clapton Orient, 1919-27

The closest that the young Tom Dixon came to professional football was an unsuccessful trial at his local Football League side, Sunderland. He was working long hours as a coal miner and playing for various amateur sides in the Sunderland & District League. At this time, Clapton Orient prided itself on its scouting network, which found the North-East area a rich vein of talent. A contact of the respected O's manager, Billy 'Doc' Holmes, recommended the young wing-half he had seen in a local game and a trial was arranged.

Tommy Dixon was promptly offered a contract and added to the first-team squad. His first two seasons at Millfields Road saw him failing to gain a regular place in the starting eleven, however, due mainly to the fine form of the veteran pairing of Jack Forrest and Joe Nicholson. When Forrest left for Northampton, Dixon seized his chance and became a fixture at right-half for the next six seasons. His greatest performance in an Orient shirt came in February 1925, when his driving industry in the middle of the park galvanised The O's to a remarkable 2-0 FA Cup victory over mighty Newcastle United. Dixon also gave Orient several sterling performances as a forward. His consistency and hard work drew admiring glances from several rival managers

but, in June 1927, it was Ted Birnie who tempted Dixon away from East London.

Dixon was to prove a very astute signing for Southend, missing very few games over the next seven seasons and forming a redoubtable midfield triumvirate with Joe Wilson and Dickie Donoven. In the 1928/29 season, Dixon played in every match for Southend and his efforts in midfield led to many goals for Jimmy Shankly during his record breaking 35-goal haul that term.

Tommy Dixon made his 250th appearance for Southend in January 1934, against Coventry at Highfield Road. Shortly afterwards, now thirty-four years old, he announced that he would retire at the end of the season. It was a testimony to his presence in the side that Southend would have to turn to the Republic of Ireland captain, Charlie Turner, to find an adequate replacement.

Dickie Donoven
Striker/Midfielder

Born: Bulwell, Nottinghamshire, 20/6/1900

Joined: July 1925, from Mansfield

First team debut: v. Reading, 5/9/25

Appearances: 332

Goals: 58

Other clubs: Bulwell, 1917-20; Nottingham Forest, 1920-21; Mansfield, 1922-25

Dickie Donoven came to the fore as a prolific scorer at youth level for Bulwell Schoolboys. It was no surprise that he attracted the interest of several League clubs and it was Nottingham Forest manager, Bob Masters, who won the race for his signature. At the age of nineteen, he was offered professional terms at the City Ground. He was unable to gain a regular first-team place, but performed exceptionally in the reserve team.

Donoven's desire for first-team football meant that Masters reluctantly let him move to Mansfield Town in May 1922. The Stags were a formidable outfit and Donoven soon became a crowd favourite, forming a prodigious partnership with George 'Baby' Greatorex in the 1922/23 campaign. Donoven scored 14 League goals and played a major part in Town's Notts Senior Cup victory that year. The next season, Greatorex was allowed to leave and Baynes, the Mansfield manager, saw Donoven as his main source for goals. The diminutive Donoven rose to the challenge by scoring 36 goals in 42 matches as Mansfield won the Midland League championship. The title was retained the following season, with Donoven upping his personal contribution to 37 goals in just 37 games.

Ted Birnie, the Southend manager at the time, decided that Donoven's return to the Football League was overdue and paid the Field Mill club £500 for their star forward in May

1925. He scored in only his second game but was initially unable to break the regular partnership of Billy Hick and William Shaw. However, Shaw moved on to Gainsborough Trinity in the summer of 1926 and Donoven became Hick's regular partner in attack.

In the 1926/27 campaign, Donoven scored 17 goals and his incisive and shrewd play set up many of Billy Hick's new club record of 29 goals in a season. Over the next three seasons, Donoven contributed respectable double-figure goal tallies in each campaign. In the summer of 1930, Ted Birnie announced that his forward line for the new season would be Jimmy Shankly, Arthur Crompton and Fred Barnett and that he saw Donoven's future as a wing-half. Donoven had never played in that position before but Birnie's decision was to prove an astute one.

Dickie Donoven became the first Blues player to reach 300 appearances for the club when he played against Bournemouth & Boscombe Athletic at The Kursaal in October 1933. The 1934/35 campaign saw David Jack take over as manager and he brought in a new wing-half, Billy Carr, from Huddersfield Town. Donoven only appeared seven times during that campaign and, at the end of the season, he announced his retirement – a month before his thirty-fifth birthday and after 332 appearances in a Southend United shirt.

Frank Dudley
Striker

Born: Southend-on-Sea, Essex, 9/5/1925

Joined: August 1945, from local football

First team debut: v. Watford, 17/11/45

Appearances: 92

Goals: 33

Other clubs: Leeds, 1949-51; Southampton, 1951-53; Cardiff, 1953-54; Brentford, 1954-56

Frank Dudley caught the eye of Southend manager Harry Warren as an inside forward with 1312 Squadron of the Air Training Cadets and was invited for a trial at the Southend Stadium in September 1945. A month later he signed professional terms with the club. Dudley was a spiky, blond, big-boned centre forward, who achieved his lifetime ambition by playing for the team he supported as a child. Respected as a glutton for work on the pitch as much as for his undying enthusiasm for the game, Frank played for five League clubs during his career and scored goals for all of them.

His three years at Southend produced 33 goals, including two hat-tricks – against Northampton Town in March 1947 and at Exeter City three weeks later. In the summer of 1949, he moved to then Second Division Leeds United for a club record fee of £10,000, with Albert Wakefield moving to The Blues as part of the deal. In his first season at Elland Road, he top scored with 16 League and cup goals. He scored another 11 times in the 1950/51 season before joining Southampton in February 1951, whilst onboard a Leeds-London express train. The deal saw Ernie Stephenson move in the opposite direction.

After managing a goal ratio of almost a goal every other game for The Saints (32 goals in 67 appearances), Frank spent three months with Cardiff City before moving to Brentford in December 1953. He achieved a remarkable feat in the 1953/54 campaign when his first three League goals of the season came for three different clubs in three different divisions. The first was for Southampton (in the Third Division (South)), the second was for Cardiff City (in the First Division) and the third was for Brentford (Second Division). It was at Griffin Park that Frank Dudley played out the last matches of a professional career which spanned over 300 matches and produced nearly 120 goals.

On leaving professional football in 1958, Dudley spent a couple of seasons winding down his playing career with Folkestone Town. Having already qualified as a coach back in 1952, he rejoined Southend United as youth team manager in 1961, a post he kept until 1965. He then served in local government in the town until his retirement in 1985. He is still a regular supporter in the East Stand at Roots Hall, along with ex-colleagues of the late 1940s – Joe Sibley, Jack French and his replacement in The Shrimpers' forward line, Albert Wakefield. He still lives in the town and is a shareholder in his beloved hometown club.

Dave Elliott
Midfielder

Born: Tantobie, Co. Durham, 10/2/1945

Joined: February 1971, from Newcastle

First team debut: v. Stockport, 19/2/71

Appearances: 189(4)

Goals: 9

Other clubs: Sunderland, 1962-66, Newcastle, 1966-70; Newport County, 1975-78

After leaving school at the age of fifteen, Dave joined Northern Counties League Gateshead, who had recently failed to gain re-election to the Football League, having been voted out in 1960. After a highly impressive season at Redheugh Park, Elliott was offered an apprenticeship at Sunderland.

His progress at Roker Park was rapid and his manager, Alan Brown, offered him professional terms when he turned seventeen. In December 1966, after 30 League appearances and 1 goal, Dave swapped the red and white of Wearside for the black and white of their fiercest rivals, Newcastle United. He earned himself a fairly regular first-team place, including The Magpies' Fairs Cup success of 1969. Having played in most of the earlier rounds, Dave was a travelling substitute for the first leg of the final in Hungary against Ujpest Dozsa. A 3-2 away win followed by a 3-0 success at St James Park meant that he was the proud owner of a winners medal for a European competition. Coincidentally, one of the Newcastle goals in the home leg was scored by Alan Foggon, who went on to make 26 appearances for The Blues during the 1977/78 season.

Dave Elliott joined Southend in February 1971, just twenty-four hours after The Shrimpers had signed his old Newcastle team-mate, Terry Johnson. The pair quickly resumed the on-field understanding that had flourished so well in the North East. Despite making nearly 200 appearances, and showing no little toil and effort, Elliott never truly won over all sections of the Roots Hall crowd.

He left the club in July 1975 to join Newport County as player-manager, but his first step in management did not last long as he was sacked ten months later. However, shortly afterwards he obtained a similar position at Bangor City. After taking the Welsh side to within one match of European football, his side losing 3-1 to Wrexham in the 1978 Welsh Cup final, he returned to Somerton Park for a second, even briefer, spell in charge of Newport County. He subsequently returned to Bangor City and guided the Farrar Road side with considerable success.

In 1981, his side reached the semi-final of the FA Trophy and a year later they won the Northern Premier League championship. After a season in the Alliance Premier League, however, they were relegated and Elliott departed for a second time. Since those days he has held coaching posts at Cardiff City and Caernarfon Town.

Jimmy Evans
Defender

Born: Rhyl, Clwyd, 29/12/1894

Joined: August 1919, from Ton Pentre

First team debut: v. Brighton, 4/9/1920

Appearances: 132

Goals: 15

Other clubs: Ton Pentre, 1913-15; Rhyl, 1918-19; Burnley, 1922-25; Swansea, 1925-26; Rhyl, 1926-32

Although born in North Wales, Jimmy Evans carved out his early playing career in the southern Welsh valleys with Ton Pentre. After serving in the First World War, he was playing for his hometown side, Rhyl, but was looking to join a professional club and, in August 1919, he signed for Southend. The club had a moderately successful season in the Southern League First Division, finishing in mid-table, and Evans played in about half the League fixtures and the two FA Cup ties against Watford and Sheffield United, the latter in front of a 40,000 crowd at Bramall Lane.

In May 1920 Southend, now under Tom Mather's management, gained election to the Football League and Evans played the majority of matches in that inaugural season. The 1921/22 campaign saw Evans play all but two matches, when Billy Evans deputised. It was a desperate season for The Blues, who finished bottom of the Third Division (South). Southend's plight had been compounded by a lack of goals with Evans being the clubs' leading scorer with 10. All these strikes came from the spot and his remarkable run of penalty successes included five in six matches. Evans' unusual method for spot kicks would see him signal to the referee from his defensive position, before swooping in and, without stopping, strike the ball into the net with tremendous force.

His excellent form in a struggling side saw Evans become Southend's second player to gain international recognition, following in the footsteps of Lot Jones. Evans played for Wales in all three British Championship matches of 1922 and gained a fourth cap against Scotland in March 1923. His first two games at international level, against Scotland and England, saw him gain rave reviews despite being played out of position at right-back, the left-back berth taken by Cardiff's Bert Evans. The 1922/23 season under Ted Birnie was slightly more successful, with The Blues in mid-table. Evans added four more penalty conversions to his tally and scored his only Southend goal from open play when he netted in a 5-0 triumph over Exeter City.

In April 1923, Birnie reluctantly sold his prized asset to Burnley for £1,000. However, Evans was to struggle at Turf Moor, finding the rigours of First Division football too much and in his two full seasons at Burnley, he was really only a bit-part player. He returned to South Wales with Second Division Swansea Town for a final League campaign in 1925/26. Evans then rejoined his hometown side, Rhyl, for whom he played for another six seasons before retiring in 1932, aged thirty-eight. He then managed the Rhyl Supporters Social Club for thirty years until his retirement. Jimmy Evans died in his native Clwyd in 1975 at the age of eighty.

Eddie Firmani
Striker

Born: Cape Town, South Africa, 7/8/1933

Joined: June 1965, from Charlton Athletic

First team debut: v. Swansea, 21/8/65

Appearances: 62

Goals: 28

Other clubs: Clyde (South Africa), 1949-51; Charlton Athletic, 1951-54, 1963-65 & 1966-67; Sampdoria (Italy), 1955-58; Internazionale (Italy), 1958-62; Genoa (Italy), 1962-63; Tampa Bay Rowdies (USA), 1975

Eddie Firmani was born in Cape Town, South Africa and began his football career with local side, Clyde. The Charlton Athletic manager, Jimmy Seed, took a chance on the frail-looking youngster in the summer of 1951. Firmani grabbed the chance to shine and rewarded Seed's faith in his ability with 50 goals in 100 games over the following three seasons.

Having Italian ancestry, Firmani had dual nationality and moved to Italy with Sampdoria for the 1955/56 season. After a highly successful time there, Internazionale paid a staggering £88,000 for his services for the 1958/59 campaign. Firmani had immediate impact, scoring 20 times in 30 matches, as Inter improved their League position from eleventh in the previous campaign to third, only six points adrift of champions and city rivals AC Milan, and was equally successful in the next two seasons with Inter. Firmani ended his Italian adventures with a less successful stint at Genoa, but still finished with outstanding career figures in Serie A of 107 goals in only 194 matches.

Firmani utilised his Italian parentage to play for Italy on three occasions. He scored on his international debut in November 1956 as Italy drew 1-1 with Switzerland in Basle. He gained further caps against Northern Ireland in 1957 and Austria a year later, but was unable to displace Giampiero Boniperti and Gino Pivatelli as a regular in the national side.

He returned to England for the 1963/64 season, rejoining Charlton Athletic, and in August 1965, Southend United manager Alvan Williams splashed out a new club record fee of £10,000 for the mercurial talent. In his first season at Roots Hall, he top scored with 20 goals from 42 matches, despite Southend suffering relegation to the Fourth Division. In the 1966/67 season, Firmani found himself being left out of the side on a regular basis, and found himself increasingly at odds with the rest of the squad. The dispute worsened when the other players learned of Firmani's salary – which was considerably more than their own. In March 1967, Alvan Williams decided to cut his losses and Firmani was sold back to Charlton where he also succeeded Bob Stokoe as manager.

In the mid-1970s, Firmani moved to the United States as a successful coach, first of the Tampa Bay Rowdies and then the New York Cosmos, in the North American Soccer League. Firmani subsequently spent many years involved in the game in the States, most recently as coach of Major Soccer League side New York/New Jersey Metrostars.

Andy Ford
Defender

Born: Minehead, Somerset, 4/5/1954

Joined: May 1973, from Bournemouth

First team debut: v. Blackburn Rovers, 25/8/73

Appearances: 152(3)

Goals: 2

Other clubs: Minehead, 1970-72; Bournemouth, 1972-73; Swindon, 1977-79; Gillingham, 1980-82

After leading his local league team, Minehead, onto the pitch as a mascot, Andy followed that up by playing for the club and, having captained Somerset's schools and under-18 teams, he joined his first League club aged seventeen.

It was Bournemouth who had snapped the youngster up, but after two years, Andy was given a free transfer. On 4 May 1973, he joined the staff at Roots Hall, and made his debut at left-back in the opening game of the 1973/74 season, a 0-1 defeat at Ewood Park against Blackburn Rovers. Andy made the position his own for the campaign, missing out only when injured, and opened his scoring account in a 2-3 away defeat to Cambridge United in January 1974. The following season, 1974/75, Andy managed another goal, but didn't have it all his own way, having to share the number three shirt with Bob Worthington and Tony Taylor.

The 1975/76 season proved different though, and Andy's tough tackling and work rate earned him the left-back spot from the start of October until the end of the season, with 46 appearances in all. The 1976/77 season proved to be the highlight of Andy's Blues career, as he played in every single game of the season, 52 in all, but his consistency proved attractive to other clubs and Swindon Town came in for him. Finding the Third Division and a move back towards home

an attractive proposition, Andy joined the County Ground team, and found himself in the same side as another Southend favourite, Chris Guthrie.

After flitting in and out of the side for the first half of the season, Andy wrestled the left-back spot from old stalwart John Trollope, who had made over 700 League appearances for Swindon in that position. Andy's performances the next season, 1978/79, were so good that John Trollope had to move to right-back, and Andy was an ever-present in a team that missed out on promotion to the Second Division by just three points. The 1979/80 season saw Andy injured after only four games, and he never managed to regain his place, eventually transferring to Gillingham in July 1980. Here, Andy found himself partnering a young Steve Bruce, and he even managed a goal on his debut for the Gills in a 1-2 opening day defeat at Exeter City.

After three seasons punctuated by injury, Andy finally retired from League football, but he settled in Kent, running his own picture-frame making business, whilst keeping himself active in the local leagues. Currently, he is manager of Ryman League side Gravesend & Northfleet.

Neil Freeman
Goalkeeper

Born: Northampton, 16/2/1955

Joined: July 1976, from Grimsby

First team debut: v. Watford, 21/8/76

Appearances: 76

Goals: 0

Other clubs: Arsenal, 1972-74; Grimsby, 1974-75; Birmingham, 1978-79; Peterborough, 1981-82; Northampton, 1982-83

Neil signed professional forms with Arsenal in June 1972 at seventeen. After twenty-one months without a first-team appearance, he signed for Grimsby Town and made his debut in a 2-0 home win over Port Vale in April 1974. The following season saw Neil sharing the goalkeeper's jersey with old Grimsby stalwart, Harry Wainman, but after making only 10 appearances in the 1975/76 season, Neil decided it was time to move on, joining Southend United in time for the opening of the 1976/77 campaign.

Neil, at 6' 2" and nearly 14 stone, proved a colossus in the Southend goal, showing considerable agility to go with his dominating size. It was no coincidence that, when Neil was injured with only ten games to go and the team sitting in the top eight and pushing for promotion, a slump in form occurred – just two wins in those final matches leaving The Blues tenth, ten points outside the promotion places.

The following season, 1977/78, saw Southend finish as runners-up to Watford in the Fourth Division. By now, some of the bigger clubs were beginning to take an interest, and it was no surprise when Birmingham City of the First Division snapped him up during the close season. Although he started the 1978/79 season as

the understudy to Jim Montgomery, Neil was soon called into action as Birmingham lurched from one crisis to another. By the end of the season, Neil had made 29 appearances and conceded 41 goals, but Birmingham were relegated.

Birmingham signed Jeff Wealands during the close season before the start of the 1979/80 campaign, and that was effectively the end of Neil's St Andrews career. After playing in the 3-4 opening day defeat at home to Fulham, he made only one more appearance before leaving to join Peterborough United in September 1981, having also had brief loan spells with Walsall and Huddersfield Town. Neil played 41 League matches for Peterborough in the 1981/82 season, and they narrowly missed being promoted. The following season, however, he found himself ousted from the team by a £4,000 signing from Leeds United, a certain David Seaman.

Neil joined Northampton Town on a non-contract basis, playing 22 matches, but found the change in the laws of the game – which meant that goalkeepers were sent off for a professional foul – too much to cope with, and decided to retire as a professional footballer and become a policeman. In terms of goals conceded per game, Neil has the best record of any goalkeeper to have played 30 or more games for Southend United, conceding only 66 goals in 76 games, and he really should have gone to greater things.

John 'Jackie' French
Defender

Born: Stockton, Cleveland, 19/1/1925

Joined: February 1947, from Middlesbrough*

First team debut: v. Bristol Rovers, 8/2/47

Appearances: 198

Goals: 22

Other clubs: Middlesbrough, 1942-46; Nottingham Forest, 1952-55

At the tender age of fifteen, Jackie joined Middlesbrough from South Bank Juniors, signing as a professional in August 1945. During the war, Jackie was a gunner with 121 Training Regiment, Royal Artillery, and it was whilst serving for his country that he signed for Southend United in February 1947.

A week after being demobbed, Jackie returned to Aldershot to play for the Royal Artillery in the Army Cup final replay, filling the half-back position and acting as captain. Whilst Jackie was taking a throw-in, lightning struck and he was thrown to the ground, but apart from a curious tingling sensation through his arms and fingers, he was not affected. Tragically, two players were killed instantaneously, and four were injured; the Southend United manager, Harry Warren, was a spectator at the game.

Jackie made his League debut for The Blues in the 2-3 home defeat to Bristol Rovers in February 1947, but that proved to be his only appearance of the campaign. The 1947/48 season was not a great deal better, with Jackie managing only 2 League appearances, but he began the 1948/49 season as a first-choice player and, although he played in a variety of defensive positions during the season, he made 37 appearances in all. Jackie also opened his goalscoring account for The Blues with the only goal in the 1-0 home win over Aldershot in February 1949.

Jackie missed only two games in the 1949/50 season and played against the great Stanley Matthews in The Blues' 0-4 third round FA Cup defeat at Bloomfield Road against Blackpool. He missed only four games the following season, and as Southend notched up the biggest total of goals scored in the club's history (92), he managed five. Jackie bettered his record the following season, ending in double figures with 11 goals and finishing the 1951/52 campaign as an ever-present. He was selected by the FA to play for the England 'B' team, along with Les Stubbs, against the British Olympic XI at Highbury, and both players managed to score.

Jackie's representative honours, along with his excellent club play, sparked the interest of Nottingham Forest, and in November 1952, he joined the City Ground club. Jackie's stay in Nottingham was racked with injuries, and he made only 80 starts in nearly four years. Before the start of the 1956/57 season, Jackie re-joined Southend United, but managed only 5 appearances before his League career ended. He played with Folkestone Town, then moved into management with Basildon United. He later did some sterling work for the club and was a guiding light in the Supporters' Club.

Bill Garner

Striker

Born: Leicester, 14/12/1947

Joined: November 1969, from Bedford

First team debut: v. York, 22/11/69

Appearances: 110(1)

Goals: 47

Other clubs: Notts County, 1966-67; Bedford, 1967-79; Chelsea, 1972-78; Cambridge, 1978-80; Chelmsford, 1980-83; Brentford, 1983-84

Bill Garner played for many clubs before finally breaking into the big time with, firstly, Southend United, and then Chelsea. These teams included Leicester Victoria, Loughborough United, and Midland Athletic. Whilst with Midland Athletic, Bill represented the county in their All-England Cup-winning team, alongside future Leicester City stars David Nish and Rodney Fern.

Notts County became Bill's first professional club, when he joined them in July 1966, but he managed only two appearances before rejoining Loughborough United in the Midland League, this time as a professional. After brief spells at Dunstable and Bedford Town, Arthur Rowley signed him for Southend United.

Bill made his debut for The Blues in the 0-1 defeat at York City on 22 November 1969. The season overall was a poor one for The Blues, but Bill began forming a good partnership with Billy Best. Although the 1970/71 campaign wasn't much better for the team, Bill and Billy notched 34 goals between them, including four for Bill in one FA Cup tie at home to Weymouth. The 1971/72 season was an outstanding one for Southend United, and Bill in particular. 26 League and cup goals in 44 appearances meant that he was The Blues' top scorer for the cam-

paign. Bill scored his only League hat-trick for Southend in a 4-2 home win over Chester in March 1972, and his form in front of goal began to make the big clubs take notice.

After six matches of the 1972/73 season, Chelsea paid Southend £100,000 for Bill. He made his Chelsea debut as a substitute three days after signing, and scored his first goal on his first full appearance, on 30 September away to Coventry City. Although never quite cementing a permanent first-team place, Bill scored 6 goals in 21 appearances by the end of the campaign. Bill played in only half of the League matches the following season, but still managed a respectable 7 goals. He also found himself playing alongside future Southend boss, Dave Webb. Chelsea were relegated from the First Division at the end of the 1974/75 campaign, despite Bill's 6 goals in only 15 full appearances. In 1976/77, Chelsea finished runners-up in the Second Division, but Bill didn't even make a single appearance, though he returned the following season to add 5 more goals to his total.

After only one game in the 1978/79 campaign, Bill left Stamford Bridge for a single season at Cambridge United. He then drifted into non-League football, but rejoined Brentford in 1983 as a non-contract player, making three appearances at the age of thirty-five and scoring a goal, proving that he still had the touch.

Bobby Gilfillan
Striker

Born: Cowdenbeath, Fife, 29/7/1938

Joined: July 1963, from Raith Rovers

First team debut: v. Oldham, 21/9/63

Appearances: 71(1)

Goals: 35

Other clubs: Cowdenbeath, 1957-59; Newcastle, 1959-60; Raith Rovers, 1960-63; Doncaster Rovers, 1965-70

Bobby Gilfillan's football career was distinguished by one spectacular season – thankfully, it came with Southend United. Gilfillan's career started as a youngster with his hometown side, Cowdenbeath, who were in the basement division of the Scottish Football League, and progressed via Newcastle United and Raith Rovers to Southend, signed by Ted Fenton in July 1963. Fenton's squad, however, was top heavy, with forwards including Jimmy Conway, Ray Smith, Benny Friel and Micky Beesley and at first Gilfillan could not hold a regular place.

At the turn of the year, both Smith and Conway missed games through injury and Gilfillan made the most of his opportunity, scoring regularly until the end of the campaign, including four goals in a 7-1 demolition of Shrewsbury – making him the first Southend player to hit four in a game since Bud Houghton achieved the feat in a match at Mansfield in April 1959. Gilfillan's outstanding season came in 1964/65, which would, coincidentally, be Ted Fenton's last in charge of The Blues. The Scotsman top scored with 22 League goals, which was a remarkable achievement as he did not open his account until October when he scored against Gillingham. In the same month he hit all three goals against Workington and kicked off November by again scoring four goals in a game; this time Colchester fell victim to a rampant Gilfillan as Southend triumphed 6-3 in a thrilling Essex derby. He also scored braces against Reading, Grimsby and in both games versus Oldham. Gilfillan finished a stunning season well clear of the next best Southend goalscorer, John McKinven, who managed 11.

Southend started the 1965/66 season with a new manager, Alvan Williams, who invested a club record £10,000 on a new striker, the vastly experienced Eddie Firmani. Williams made it clear that Gilfillan was no longer part of his plans and offloaded the striker to Doncaster Rovers in November 1968. However, his last months at the club were notable for his becoming the first-ever Southend substitute when he replaced Bobby King in a match at Walsall, following the introduction of the new rule allowing teams one reserve per game. Gilfillan would serve Doncaster for five seasons but, although a more than useful performer, he would never recapture the prolific goalscoring touch he enjoyed in that one spectacular season.

Billy Goodwin
Striker

Born: Staveley, Derbyshire, c. 1892

Joined: July 1922, from Manchester Utd

First team debut: v. Newport County, 26/8/1922

Appearances: 91

Goals: 35

Other clubs: Old Staveley Primitives, 1908-10; Chesterfield Town, 1910-13 & 1915-17; Blackburn Rovers, 1913-14; Exeter, 1914-15 & 1919-20; Manchester Utd, 1920-22; Dartford, 1928-29

Billy Goodwin was born in Staveley and first played football for his local amateur side, Old Staveley Primitives. He came to the attention of the strongest club in the area, Chesterfield Town, and joined them in 1910. However, Town would disband in 1917, following an investigation into financial irregularities. Goodwin never made the first team, but scored prolifically for the reserves and gained a lucrative move to Blackburn Rovers in March 1913.

He found the move up to Football League level too much at that stage, however, and after scoring a hat-trick in a practice match for Exeter City, he stepped down to the Southern League. Goodwin scored on his Exeter debut against West Ham United in September 1914 and found the net eleven times in his first eleven matches for The Grecians. Goodwin finished the 1914/15 campaign with 23 goals from 36 games, which broke Exeter's club record and remained unbeaten until the 1926/27 season. Goodwin missed the final two games of the 1914/15 season after he badly dislocated his elbow.

Goodwin went on to rejoin Chesterfield Town. He scored prolifically in both seasons at Saltergate but returned to Exeter for the 1919/20 season, scoring 17 goals. In June 1920, John Robson brought him to Manchester United. In his first season at Old Trafford, Goodwin scored once in 5 appearances for the first team. He was

also selected by the Central League to face the North Eastern League in a representative match at Newcastle in January 1921. The next season Goodwin played two of the first three games of the campaign, but, by October 1921, John Robson was replaced by John Chapman and Goodwin was never picked again.

Billy Goodwin joined Southend in August 1922 and repaid manager Ted Birnie's faith in him by finishing the campaign as leading marksman with 22 goals from 44 matches. The 1923/24 season saw a less-prolific Goodwin, who found the net only 11 times in 39 games, before his season ended abruptly in April when he sustained a badly broken leg. The injury was to effectively end his career, although he attempted a comeback in the winter of 1926. After a few games, he had to accept the fact that he was no longer able to withstand the rigours of the full-time game.

A benefit game against Brentford was arranged for him at the start of the next season, by which time he had joined non-League Dartford. Goodwin used the money from his well-attended benefit match to set up a wholesale confectionery business in Princes Street, Southend. Affectionately named The United Confectionery Sweet Factory, the firm remained in the town for many years, as did Goodwin, who passed away in the 1960s.

Cyril Grant
Striker

Born: Wath-on-Dearne, South Yorkshire, 10/7/1920

Joined: March 1948, from Fulham

First team debut: v. Aldershot, 20/3/48

Appearances: 183

Goals: 64

Other clubs: Mexborough, 1936-39; Lincoln, 1939-46; Arsenal, 1946-47; Fulham, 1947-48; Gravesend & Northfleet, 1955-57

Although born in the Yorkshire village of Wath, Cyril called Mexborough his home. At the young age of seventeen, he joined Wolverhampton Wanderers as an outside right, but, after only a brief stay at Molineux, moved to Lincoln City. Unfortunately for him, he signed for The Imps in June 1939, which meant that his League career had to take a backseat due to the Second World War.

Cyril spent five years in the Navy, and it was there that he successfully converted into a centre forward. Whilst stationed at Hull, Cyril had a phenomenal spell of goalscoring – notching hat-tricks in no less than nine consecutive games, and scoring sixty goals in the space of four months. In July 1946, still before he had made a League appearance, Arsenal signed Cyril from Lincoln City. Grant had scored 5 times for The Imps in 10 wartime matches, having rejoined the Sincil Bank club in January 1946. Cyril finally made his League debut at the age of twenty-six, but unfortunately he managed only one further start in The Gunners' first team, before a move across London to Fulham. Fifteen months at Craven Cottage brought 4 goals in 14 games, before a move in March 1948 to join Southend United.

It was at this point in his career that Cyril really found his feet. He marked his Blues debut with the third goal in a 4-0 victory at home to Aldershot, and he finished his first full season with The Blues (1948/49) as second top scorer behind Frank Dudley, managing 9 goals in only 26 appearances. The 1949/50 season was a difficult one for Cyril, and he found it nearly impossible to wrestle a first-team place from the impressive Albert Wakefield. Wakefield's return of 28 goals in 42 matches meant that Cyril spent most of the season in the reserves, and it wasn't until halfway through the 1950/51 campaign that he finally won the number nine shirt back, finishing with 12 goals from 26 appearances.

The following season was Cyril's most successful for The Blues in terms of goals scored, the 18 he managed in 47 League and cup games leaving him level with Les Stubbs and only three behind the top scorer, his old adversary, Albert Wakefield. The 1952/53 campaign saw Cyril finally claim the top scorer for the season award, scoring 13 in 39 appearances, but this proved to be the zenith of his Blues career. After two more seasons, Cyril retired from League action, his final appearance coming in the 3-2 victory over Brentford on 30 April 1955, at the age of thirty four. He rounded off his playing career with a few appearances for Gravesend & Northfleet. Cyril's final record for Southend, of 64 goals in 183 League and cup appearances, marks him out as one of the best to pull on the blue shirt during a period in which the club seemed to score goals for fun.

Terry Gray
Midfielder

Born: Bradford, West Yorkshire, 3/6/1954

Joined: July 1979, from Huddersfield

First team debut: v. Brentford, 15/8/79

Appearances: 119(4)

Goals: 30

Other clubs: Leeds Ashley Road, 1970-72; Huddersfield, 1972-28; Bradford, 1982-84; Preston North End, 1984-85

Terry Gray was a good performer both in and out of the classroom. He gained an 'A' level and eleven 'O' levels and also represented England at both schoolboy and youth level. As if that was not enough, the youngster also reached the third round of the junior tennis tournament at Wimbledon. Finally, he signed associate schoolboy forms for Chelsea, but was soon released by the London club, returning to his home county and playing Yorkshire League football for Leeds Ashley Road.

It was during his stay at Ashley Road that the Huddersfield Town manager, Ian Greaves, spotted Terry's potential and signed him as a professional in August 1972. It was the 1973/74 season before he made his first-team debut for The Terriers. Unfortunately for Terry, he was asked to play in an unfamiliar left-back position. Terry eventually found himself his usual attacking midfield role, and opened his goalscoring account in March 1974. The 1974/75 season saw Terry in and out of the team, but in 1975/76 he really found his goalscoring boots, netting 15 goals in only 29 League matches and finished top scorer, despite breaking his leg.

Terry didn't manage to get his place back in the Huddersfield team on a regular basis until March 1977. The 1977/78 season was one of his best, as he missed only one League game and scored 10 times. However, he was beginning to feel that his career needed a change, and moved on to join Southend United.

Although Southend ended the 1979/80 season with relegation, Terry showed what he was capable of. If that season was poor, by contrast the 1980/81 season was a massive triumph. The side stormed to the Fourth Division championship, and Terry claimed 17 of the 79 goals scored in League matches. That campaign proved to be a difficult act to follow, and Terry could not rise to the standard he had previously set himself. In August 1982, he moved back north to join Bradford City.

After two seasons, Terry found himself on the move again, this time to Preston North End. However, North End were facing hard times and his first season at Deepdale coincided with Preston's relegation to the Fourth Division. During the ill-fated campaign he only appeared in 13 matches and failed to find the net. The 1985/86 season was even worse as Preston finished next to bottom in the Football League's basement division.

Terry's League career came to an end during the summer of 1986, having scored a total of 80 goals. While his career ended on a low note, he will always have good memories of the substantial part he played in Southend's only championship-winning team. He currently lives in Yorkshire, and works in the insurance industry.

Chris Guthrie
Striker

Born: Hexham, Northumberland, 7/9/1953

Joined: November 1972, from Newcastle

First team debut: v. Bristol Rovers, 24/11/1972

Appearances: 117(1)

Goals: 40

Other clubs: Newcastle, 1970-71; Sheffield Utd, 1975-77; Swindon, 1977-78; Fulham, 1978-79; Millwall, 1979-80

After making 7 appearances for England schoolboys and scoring 6 goals, Chris achieved his lifelong ambition in January 1971, signing as a professional for his childhood heroes, Newcastle United. However, things turned sour after only three appearances for The Magpies, and Chris signed for The Blues in 1972.

Chris was the perfect replacement for Bill Garner, who had left the Hall earlier in the season for Chelsea. It only took three games for Chris to open his Southend account, and by the end of the season he was top scorer with 15 goals in only 25 appearances. Although not as prolific the following season, Chris struck up an excellent partnership with the diminutive Stuart Brace, helping Stuart notch 22 goals to his own 8 during the 1973/74 season.

By now, Chris' strength and guile were attracting admiring glances from other clubs, and after he finished the 1974/75 campaign as Southend's top scorer again, this time with 17 goals in 48 appearances, the chequebooks came out and Chris left for Sheffield United. Unfortunately for Chris, his first season in the First Division also proved to be his last. Although he managed 9 goals in his 39 League appearances, Sheffield United finished bottom of the table and were relegated. Chris's first goal for The Blades was in front of nearly 56,000 people at Old Trafford – but it was a consolation goal in a 1-5 defeat. Sheffield United won only six matches all season, although Chris managed a goal in five of those.

A mid-table finish in the Second Division the next season ended with Chris moving from Bramall Lane to Third Division Swindon Town. After scoring on his debut for The Robins, Chris went on to score 12 goals in 39 appearances, but after only seven games of the 1978/79 season, he was off again, this time to Fulham. This proved a much more successful move for Chris, and he finished the campaign as Fulham's top scorer, with 13 goals in 34 appearances. The 1979/80 season was a poor one for Fulham, which ended in relegation to the Third Division. Chris played for the first half of the campaign, but managed only two goals, before being transferred to another London side, Millwall, in March 1980. After scoring on his home debut at The Den, Chris never managed to recapture his old form, and he left The Lions at the end of the season.

During the 1991/92 season, after nearly twenty years away from Newcastle United, Chris was appointed kit man at St James's Park, giving him the chance to once more serve the club he loved.

Tony Hadley
Defender/Midfielder

Born: Rochford, Essex, 5/7/1955

Joined: July 1974, from Basildon*

First team debut: v. Grimsby, 29/11/1974

Appearances: 313(24)

Goals: 21

Other clubs: Basildon Utd, 1972-74; Colchester Utd, 1983-84

Tony signed full professional forms with Southend in July 1974 and made his first-team debut four months later in a 3-0 defeat of Grimsby Town. The 1975/76 season was the campaign in which Tony became a regular first-team player, replacing the departed Neil Townsend in the centre of defence. However, despite his personal progress, The Blues were relegated to the Fourth Division at the end of the campaign. By now, Tony was becoming known as a versatile and skilful player, and it was no surprise to find him filling many different roles during the next four seasons. His natural ability in any position meant he rarely let the side down.

Tony finally opened his goalscoring account during 1976/77, when he netted an extra time winner in an FA Cup first round replay against Exeter City. He also opened the scoring in a 3-0 defeat of Newport County in the next round, and contributed four goals in League matches. During the promotion-winning season of 1977/78, Tony switched regularly between centre-back and midfield, but in the 1979/80 campaign, which resulted in another relegation, he wore no less than seven different shirt numbers during the course of the season. By the time the

memorable 1980/81 campaign came round, he was an integral part of a formidable midfield quartet alongside Anton Otulakowski, Terry Gray and Ronnie Pountney. He participated in all but two matches that season, scoring seven times in their successful promotion bid. It was back to chop and change for Tony during the next two seasons, as The Blues struggled to find their form in the higher division.

Surprisingly, he was allowed to leave at the end of the 1982/83 season, joining archrivals Colchester United. Playing under Cyril Lea at Layer Road, Tony featured in every match, with the exception of a 6-0 home triumph over Hartlepool. However, the lure of his first love was too great, and, after a solitary campaign with United – in which they finished a respectable eighth in the Fourth Division – he returned to Roots Hall for a final season in his familiar utility role. After a dismal season during 1984/85, one of the worst in the clubs' history, manager Bobby Moore released many players, including Tony, Ronnie Pountney and Lil Fuccillo. In the summer he signed, along with Pountney, for Southern League Chelmsford City.

Since his playing career ended, Tony has worked for British Rail on the Fenchurch Street line. A player who was really too skilful to be a centre-back, he will be remembered as one of Southend's most versatile players.

Harold Halse

Striker

Born: Stratford, East London, 1/1/1886

Died: Colchester, 25/3/1949

Joined: June 1906, from Wanstead

First team debut: v. Swindon Res, 1/9/1906

Appearances: 134

Goals: 169

Other clubs: Newportonians, 1902-03; Barking, 1903-04; Wanstead, 1904-06; Clapton Orient, 1905-06; Man. Utd, 1908-12; Aston Villa, 1912-13; Chelsea, 1913-21; Charlton Athletic, 1921-23

Undoubtedly, Harold Halse was the Stan Collymore of Southend United's inaugural season. Although small in stature, at only 5' 6", Halse scored 91 goals in 65 matches during the club's first campaign. Halse was not an outrageously skilful player, but could shoot powerfully and accurately from seemingly impossible angles.

He was born in Stratford on 1 January 1886 and first played football for the Park Road School in Wanstead. He then played for an amateur side in the South Essex League called Newportonians, who played at the Hare & Hounds ground in Leyton. He then turned out for Barking Town and Wanstead. It was while with the latter club that, in the 1905/06 season, he made 3 Football League appearances as an amateur for Clapton Orient. In June 1906, Halse joined the newly-formed Southend United. They had just gained election to the Second Division of the professional Southern League, much to the displeasure of Southend Athletic – the previously dominant side in the town. Halse was already familiar with his new surroundings, having spent the summer of 1906 playing cricket for Prittlewell.

He scored nearly 200 goals for the club by March 1908 and, straight after a match at Maidstone, he moved to Manchester United for the then maximum transfer fee of £350 plus the proceeds of a friendly between the two clubs at Roots Hall. His Southend team mate, Jimmy Axcell, also joined Manchester United at the same time, but would never feature in the first team and it was generally regarded that the £350 paid for Axcell was a means of getting around the limit set on transfer fees. The move angered supporters, but the directors pointed out that the massive fee would clear the mounting debts that threatened the club's existence.

Harold Halse scored in the first minute of his debut for Manchester United against Sheffield Wednesday in a 4-1 victory at Bank Street and, blossoming in the company of legendary names like Charlie Roberts and Billy Meredith, he won a League Championship medal in his first season. Halse was selected to represent the Football League, a great honour in those days, against the Irish League in October 1908. The match at Cliftonville saw the English side triumph 5-1, with Halse netting the fifth goal. He also won an FA Cup-winners' medal in

1909, when United defeated Bristol City 1-0 at the Crystal Palace – it was Halse's powerful shot cannoning back off the crossbar that allowed Sandy Turnbull to score the only goal of the match. In June of that year he gained his only England cap, scoring twice in an 8-1 demolition of Austria in Vienna.

In the Charity Shield match of 1911, Halse scored an amazing double hat-trick when United beat Swindon Town 8-4. Halse's six goals came consecutively, and he was heard taunting the shell-shocked Town 'keeper by saying 'I'll be back in a minute' after each goal. The legendary United player, Billy Meredith, said of that game that 'nobody but Halse could get a kick of the ball'. In October 1911, he was again asked to represent the Football League in two matches arranged for that month. The first was a 2-1 victory over a Southern League XI at Stoke's Victoria Ground and, five days later, a 4-0 win over their Irish counterparts was achieved at Anfield. In his last few seasons at Old Trafford, Halse was joined in the side by one of his old Southend colleagues, Samuel 'Prince' Blott, who arrived from Roots Hall in May 1909.

Halse moved on to Aston Villa in July 1912 for a fee of £1,200. He again played for the Football League XI in March 1913, although his side went down 4-1 to the Scottish League at Hampden Park. Halse played in two more FA Cup finals – becoming the first player to play in three finals for three different clubs. In 1913, he was in the triumphant Aston Villa side that defeated Sunderland 1-0 at Crystal Palace. Two years later, with Chelsea, he got to the final again – which was, ironically, to be staged at Old Trafford. This time it was to be a runners-up medal for Halse as the London side were well beaten by Sheffield United to the tune of 3-0. He had also represented the Football League for a fifth time in October 1914, when the Southern League were beaten 2-1 at Highbury.

His playing career ended with a spell back at Clapton Orient and then finally with Charlton Athletic, for whom he later scouted. In 1949, aged sixty-three, Harold Halse died at his home in Colchester.

Ian 'Chico' Hamilton
Midfielder/Striker

Born: Streatham, South London, 31/10/1950

Joined: September 1968, from Chelsea

First team debut: v. Bournemouth, 13/8/68

Appearances: 38(2)

Goals: 12

Other clubs: Chelsea, 1966-68; Aston Villa, 1969-75; Sheffield Utd, 1976-78; Minnesota Kicks (USA), 1978-81; San Jose Earthquakes (USA), 1982

Ian Hamilton was first discovered by then Chelsea coach Dave Sexton playing for his London school, and signed for Chelsea at the age of fifteen. He was given the nickname of 'Chico' by Sexton himself, who thought the youngster was 'cheeky'. Hamilton became the youngest ever player to play for Chelsea in the First Division when manager Tommy Docherty picked him to appear at White Hart Lane against Tottenham in March 1967.

Although he was selected to play for England youth and would also score two goals in his first three appearances for the Stamford Bridge side, Hamilton could not force his way into the first team on a regular basis. When the Southend manager, Ernie Shepherd, offered him regular first-team football at Roots Hall, Hamilton jumped at the chance. The 1968/69 season saw Hamilton finish as third top scorer, behind the prolific pairing of Billy Best (31 goals) and Gary Moore (21). Chico developed a strange phobia about wearing the number eleven shirt; eleven appearances wearing that number jersey brought only one goal, while twenty-four games in the number ten shirt saw him score ten times!

Chico's peculiar aversion did not put off Aston Villa, who paid Southend a record transfer fee of £40,000 for the player. At Villa Park, Chico developed even greater flair and became a huge crowd favourite. The 1970/71 season saw

Hamilton finish as joint top League goalscorer, bagging 9. When Villa finished runners-up to Manchester United in 1974/75, Hamilton scored 10 of Villa's 79 goals. He also made an appearance in a Wembley final that season, as Villa defeated Norwich City 1-0 in the League Cup final. In his seven-year stay in the Midlands, Chico made over 200 League and cup appearances, scoring more than 40 goals. He then moved north to join Sheffield United, where he stayed for two years, leaving in January 1978.

At twenty-seven, Hamilton joined the growing exodus of Football League players to the booming North American Soccer League. He spent four enjoyable campaigns with Minnesota Kicks. In his first two seasons in the States, Hamilton helped his club win the National Conference Central Division. In 1982, he joined San Jose Earthquakes but his new side struggled. When a new coach was brought in, Hamilton was replaced in the side by the signing of Canadian Mike Stojanovic. However, with Hamilton dropped from the roster, San Jose lost eleven of their remaining thirteen matches.

He was unable to secure a contract with a new club for the 1983 season and, at the relatively young age of thirty-two, decided to retire from the professional game.

Albert 'Ted' Hankey

Goalkeeper

Born: Stoke-on-Trent, Staffordshire, 24/5/1914

Died: Waterlooville, September 1998

Joined: June 1937, from the army

First team debut: v. Walsall, 22/1/1938

Appearances: 134

Goals: 0

Other clubs: Tonbridge, 1950-52

Ted Hankey was a legendary goalkeeper at Southend United, his only League club. He made 134 appearances, becoming a renowned and brave shot-stopper, as well as a hugely popular character with the fans. Ted was from the Potteries and went to school with Stanley Matthews in Hanley, playing both with and against the great man in Stoke & District schools football.

Ted's prowess between the sticks came to light when he was serving with the Royal Artillery in Aldershot. In 1935, he was selected to play in goal for the Army against the mighty Aston Villa, and although beaten four times, the newspapers of the next day reported headlines such as 'Army Custodian As Hero' and 'Hankey Keeps The Villa Score Down'. He was also a member of the 10th Field Brigade team that won the Army Cup in 1936.

Ted played a few games for The Shrimpers before the Second World War, making his debut in January 1938, but rejoined the Army for the duration of hostilities and was part of the Dunkirk evacuation, being rescued from the sea by a paddle steamer – a vessel which he regularly visited to admire in dry dock some

fifty years on. Ted was again selected for the Army XI in 1942, and played in the same team as such football legends as Stan Cullis, Tommy Lawton, Denis Compton, Jimmy Hagan and future Southend trainer, Wilf Copping.

He also shone at athletics, winning the 100 yards, long jump and triple jump at the Royal Artillery Sports Meeting in 1945. He played in goal for the Area Combined Services XI whilst on duty in Salonika, Greece, in 1945, losing by the odd goal in three, but saving a penalty. He was bought from the army after the war by Harry Warren and gave many stirring performances between the posts.

Ted was also an adept centre forward, and in 1947/48 played up front for the reserves against Spurs. The local paper reported that 'Hankey played equally as well as any centre forward who has worn a Southend jersey this season. He looked and moved like a first-class exponent of the game.' Ted was a central character in the legendary Southend match at Bristol Rovers in 1946. Having cut both his hands badly on a broken train window on the way to the match, manager Harry Warren played skipper Bob Jackson in goal, and informed no-one outside of the Southend dressing room. Amazingly, the team went on to a heroic 3-1 win, and the Rovers manager was very complimentary to the Southend

'keeper after the match – not knowing that the excited man swathed in bandages on the pitch congratulating his team mates was the regular stopper. The *Bristol Evening Post* gave Hankey an excellent write-up and the story passed into Southend folklore.

Ted's last game was a 2-1 home defeat against Northampton Town, on 22 April 1950. He had a benefit match against West Ham in May 1950, receiving the not-inconsiderable sum of £271. A friendly man, who was proud of his Army and Southend United links, he played for Tonbridge in Kent after he left Southend, and continued to receive rave reports of his goalkeeping skills. A pillar of the community in Waterlooville after his retirement, he worked hard for the British Legion until he passed away in the Hampshire town during 1998.

Billy Hick
Striker

Born: West Pelton, Co. Durham, 13/2/1903

Joined: March 1925, from Middlesbrough

First team debut: v. Swindon, 21/3/25

Appearances: 113

Goals: 76

Other clubs: Hartlepool, 1921-22; South Shields, 1922-23; Middlesbrough, 1923-25; Bristol City, 1928-29; Exeter, 1928-29; Grays Thurrock, Scunthorpe, 1929; Notts County 1929-30; Rotherham, 1930-32

Billy Hick was born near Chester-le-Street and started his career with Hartlepool United, the club having gained election to the new Division Three (North) for the 1921/22 season. The forward only made one appearance, however, and when Hartlepool installed a new manager, Hick was released. He moved to South Shields and although the young Hick impressed for the reserves, he could not break into the first team. Hick joined Middlesbrough in June 1923 and made 7 appearances for them, scoring 4 goals, although the season ended with relegation to the Second Division. He spent a second season at Ayresome Park, but was again used only sparingly by manager Herbert Bamlett – despite a return of 3 goals from 9 games.

Hick then moved south and joined Southend in March 1925. He immediately gained a berth in the first team, replacing Jim McClelland. Hick played out the rest of the 1925/26 season but, when the new campaign started, Hick found himself out of the team due to a burst of goalscoring from the unheralded Ernie Watkins. By November 1925, Hick had regained his place in the side and finished the season with 18 goals from 29 matches, including a brilliant hat-trick.

Ted Birnie then sold William Shaw to Gainsborough Trinity, and saw Hick as his primary source of goals. Hick responded to the challenge and, in the 1926/27 season, scored 29 goals from 41 games, beating Billy Goodwin's club record of 22 goals in the 1922/23 campaign, his haul including two hat-tricks. However, despite Hick's efforts and also those of his strike partner, Southend struggled to nineteenth place in Division Three (South). The Blues had a better campaign in 1927/28, finishing seventh, with Hick again top scoring with 26 goals including two hat-tricks. Remarkably, Hick broke his own club record by scoring in seven straight matches during this season – a feat equalled by Brett Angell in 1991/92, but never bettered.

In the close season, Ted Birnie signed Jimmy Shankly from Sheffield United and Hick was allowed to join Bristol City. After a few unsuccessful months at Ashton Gate, he moved to Exeter, where he rediscovered his scoring touch. Hick failed to settle in the West Country, however, and returned to Essex in the summer of 1929 to join non-League Grays Thurrock followed by Scunthorpe United, before Notts County offered him a return to the Football League. However, he was unable to break the regular County frontline of Harry Andrews and Tom Keetley, so he signed for Rotherham United. He spent a couple of highly productive seasons at Millmoor, before retiring in the summer of 1932. Hick's tally of 76 goals from only 113 matches, puts him in fifth place in the list of Southend United's most prolific goalscorers.

Roy Hollis
Striker

Born: Great Yarmouth, 24/12/1925

Died: 12/11/1998

Joined: February 1954, from Tottenham

First team debut: v. Shrewsbury, 27/2/54

Appearances: 260

Goals: 135

Other clubs: Great Yarmouth, 1945-47 & 1961-62; Norwich, 1947-52; Tottenham, 1952-53; Chelmsford, 1960-61; Lowestoft, 1962-63

Born on Christmas Eve 1925, Roy Hollis began his playing career with his home-town club, Great Yarmouth, before signing for his local Football League side, Norwich City, in May 1947. Roy certainly started his career as he meant to go on, scoring a hat-trick on his debut for The Canaries in a 4-2 victory against Reading at Elm Park in March 1948.

After scoring a fantastic 52 goals in only 96 League appearances for Norwich, Roy signed for the mighty Tottenham Hotspur in December 1952. Despite scoring twice in a FA Cup third round replay, in which Spurs beat Tranmere 9-1, Hollis could not dislodge the likes of Len Duquemin and Eddie Baily from the first-choice forward slots. After only four appearances in fourteen months at White Hart Lane, Roy accepted Southend manager Harry Warren's offer of a move to Essex in February 1954.

Roy scored on his Southend debut, notching the first goal in a 3-0 home victory over Shrewsbury Town, and finished the season as the club's second highest League scorer, having managed to hit the net 10 times in only 13 matches – which included a hat-trick against Walsall in April 1954. The following season, Roy's first full campaign with The Blues, saw him rattle in no less than 32 League and cup goals as an ever-present in the number nine

shirt. He scored a hat-trick in the League against his old club, Norwich, at Carrow Road and also one in the FA Cup at Bradford Park Avenue in the second round. He also scored a brace of goals on five occasions and formed a lethal partnership with Kevin Baron.

The 1955/56 season saw Roy miss only one game, a 7-2 defeat at Carrow Road, and he again top scored for The Blues, with 26 strikes in all competitions. He got another hat-trick, against Bournemouth in a 4-1 victory, but surpassed this feat by scoring four in a famous 6-3 victory against local rivals, Colchester United, at Layer Road. In the first season at the new Roots Hall ground, Southend's four forwards – Hollis, Baron, Sammy McCrory and John McGuigan – amassed 73 goals between them. By finishing top scorer in League matches again during the 1956/57 season, Roy became the first Blues player to take that accolade for three consecutive seasons – a feat since equalled by Billy Best, Derrick Parker, Steve Phillips and David Crown, but never bettered. Hollis' excellent understanding with Sammy McCrory was once again the springboard on which Southend built an excellent season.

The 1957/58 season was a strange one for Roy, for although netting a respectable 21 goals in 43 League and cup matches, he had to play second fiddle to his strike partner, McCrory, who netted an amazing 33 from the same number of games. By the time the 1958/59 season arrived, Hollis was still managing a goal every other game, scoring 17 in 35 League appearances, but the 1959/60 season would be his last at Roots Hall.

Despite maintaining his strike ratio with 9 goals in 21 games, he could not gain a regular place in the side, losing out to younger players such as Bud Houghton and Lou Costello. His final Blues appearance was in a 2-0 home victory over Reading in February 1960. Roy Hollis retired from League football that summer at the age of thirty-five. He joined Chelmsford City in June 1960 and later had a couple of seasons winding down his playing career with Great Yarmouth and also Lowestoft Town.

Although not the most elegant of centre forwards, Roy's record of 135 goals in 260 first-team matches for the Blues will probably never be bettered, leaving the gangly, stiff-legged forward at the top of the pile when the reckoning for the greatest Southend United goalscorer is added up. This Southend legend died in 1998, at the age of sixty-two.

David Jack

Striker

Born: Bolton, Lancashire, 3/4/1899

Died: London, 10/9/1958

Joined: July 1934, from Arsenal

First team debut: v. Crystal Palace, 28/11/36

Appearances: 1

Goals: 0

Other clubs: Plymouth Argyle, 1919-20; Bolton Wanderers, 1920-28; Arsenal, 1928-34

Although he only made one appearance for the club, David Jack was the most famous footballer to play for Southend United until the arrival of Eddie Firmani. He was born in Bolton in 1899, but was brought up in the Southend area as his father, Bob Jack, was manager of the Blues at the time. After leaving school, Jack took a job in the civil service and harboured no interest in a football career, having played only a few games for Plymouth Presbytarians and some representative matches for the Royal Navy.

In 1919, his father, now in charge of Plymouth Argyle, persuaded his son to join him at Home Park. After only one season, his mesmeric ball control persuaded Bolton Wanderers to sign him. Having enjoyed huge success with them, and becoming famous by scoring the first goal in the 1923 FA Cup final, the first to be staged at Wembley, he then won two England caps in 1924, before moving to Arsenal for a record transfer fee of £10,360. His move to Highbury saw him recalled to the England team and he scored in a 5-1 thrashing of France. A 3-1 win over Belgium followed. Jack captained his country 3 times in 1930, scoring in matches against Scotland and Germany, and appearing in a goalless draw against Austria.

Jack gained a third FA Cup winners' medal in 1930 and the Gunners swept to the First Division title in 1930/31. Jack scored 31 League goals in

only 35 matches, but was still 7 behind top scorer Lambert. Arsenal had to settle for second place in 1931/32, but regained the title the next season – the first in a hat-trick of League Championships for the Gunners under Chapman. Jack skippered England again in 1932 against Wales at Wrexham. His ninth and final cap came in a 4-3 win over Austria.

Jack joined Southend in the summer of 1934 as manager in succession to Ted Birnie. In spite of his age, Jack was always naturally fit and he could have made a huge contribution on the field for the Blues. However, had he done so, he would have been subject to the maximum players' wage of £8 and therefore could only turn out for Southend in friendly games. His first season in charge was not spectacular, with Southend finishing in the re-election zone. Despite optimism for the future, Southend's highest finish under Jack's leadership was tenth in 1936/37. It was during this season that Jack made his only appearance in a Blues shirt, when dispensation was granted for him to participate in an FA Cup tie at Crystal Palace, which finished 1-1.

The outbreak of the Second World War saw Jack leave football for a while, before accepting the manager's post at Middlesbrough, which he held for eight years. After leaving the game again briefly, he then rejoined Southend as a scout in 1958, shortly before his death.

Bob Jackson
Defender

Born: Cornsay, Co. Durham, 21/5/1915

Joined: July 1934, from Stanley Utd

First team debut: v. QPR, 25/4/36

Appearances: 104

Goals: 0

Other clubs: Stanley Utd, 1932-34; Folkestone, 1948-50

Southend United manager David Jack signed Bob Jackson from Northern League Stanley United in July 1934. The youngster had to wait for his chance – he performed well in the reserves, but his manager did not give him his first-team debut until April 1936. The following season was also a lean period for him, with his only appearance coming in a Division Three (South) Cup defeat against Clapton Orient.

Jackson finally began to establish himself during the 1937/38 campaign and consolidated his place during the next season. However, Jackson's promising career was put on hold due to the outbreak of war, although he played one wartime season, 1945/46, for Southend. During this unofficial campaign, Jackson registered his only goal in a Southend shirt when he converted a penalty in a 1-2 defeat at Port Vale.

The Football League restarted for the 1946/47 season – and it was during this season that Jackson cemented his place in club folklore. He was not in the eleven for the match at Bristol Rovers in October 1946, but travelled as reserve. During the train journey to Eastville, goalkeeper Ted Hankey sustained badly cut hands when attempting to force open a jammed window. Trainer Wilf Copping managed to stop the bleeding, but Hankey had to go to hospital for stitches on arrival at Bristol. Jackson, having never previously kept goal, donned Hankey's cap

and volunteered his services. Warren kept quiet and hoped the media and match officials would refrain from asking any questions.

They duly did, and the pretend 'Hankey' had a marvellous game in the face of real adversity – Walton started the game with a hand injury, Smirk suffered a cut eye, and both Thompson and Harris sustained leg injuries that would restrict their mobility. 'Hankey' was beaten early on by a viciously swerving shot from Bristol's Idris Lewis, but goals from Cyril Thompson (2) and Alf Smirk gave Southend a 3-1 half-time lead. Rovers subjected the Blues' goal to a battering in the second half, but Jackson stopped everything, earning Southend a remarkable victory. As Rovers' manager Brough Fletcher congratulated Warren on his side's triumph, he picked out the goalkeeper for particular praise. Warren took delight in revealing the ruse and that Jackson was normally a centre half!

Jackson completed that season in his accustomed position, missing only one League and one cup game. In the 1947/48 season, his last at the club, Jackson lost his place to new signing George Goodyear. Jackson showed his versatility when, on several occasions, he deputized for Doug Beach at right-back. A truly interesting career was brought to an end in the summer of 1948, when Jackson was released and signed for Kent League side Folkestone Town.

Peter Johnson
Defender

Born: Harrogate, North Yorkshire, 5/10/1958

Joined: August 1986, from Exeter

First team debut: v. Peterborough, 23/8/86

Appearances: 151

Goals: 3

Other clubs: Middlesbrough, 1976-80; Newcastle, 1980-82; Doncaster Rovers, 1982-83; Darlington, 1983-85; Whitby, 1985 & 1986; Crewe Alexandra, 1985-86; Exeter, 1986; Gillingham, 1989-91; Peterborough, 1991-92

The moment Peter Johnson scored his incredible goal at Colchester in March 1988, he guaranteed himself a place in Southend United folklore. He picked up the ball in his familiar left-back position and set off on a mazy fifty-yard diagonal run across the field. On reaching the edge of the Colchester penalty area, he switched the ball back onto his left foot and crashed an unstoppable shot past a stranded Jim Brown in the Colchester goal.

Johnson's football career began as an apprentice at Middlesbrough, before John Neal offered him a professional contract in the summer of 1976. Unfortunately, Johnson had to wait until April 1978 to get his first-team debut, but he then established a regular place in the first team during the 1978/79 campaign, when his rival for the left-back slot, Ian Bailey, was injured in December and missed five months of the season. He spent one more full season at Ayresome Park before joining Second Division Newcastle United in October 1980 for £60,000. He immediately slotted into the left-back role and he formed a good left-flank partnership with a young Chris Waddle, who was in his first League campaign. However, in February 1981, Johnson lost his place to Ian Davies and never played for The Magpies again.

He did not re-emerge until October 1982, when he played 20 games in a loan spell at Bristol City,

but in March 1983, he quit St James Park for good, joining Doncaster Rovers on a free transfer. However, it was not long before he moved again, joining Darlington in August 1983. Johnson appeared in all but two games that season and he finally broke his duck on the scoring front, netting the only goal against Tranmere. In the 1984/85 season, he again was a regular in the side but was given a free transfer at the end of the campaign. As Johnson found no offers forthcoming, he opted to join Northern League Whitby Town.

In October 1985, Crewe manager Dario Gradi brought him back into League football, before he rejoined Whitby in January 1986. Two months later he had a brief stint at Exeter. In the summer of 1986 he joined the Blues and played a pivotal part in David Webb's revolution. His consistency and tenacious attacking saw him become a crowd favourite at Roots Hall. Johnson missed only 11 League matches in his three seasons at the club, but with David Webb putting his faith in the youthful Justin Edinburgh, Johnson was allowed to leave in the summer of 1989. He spent two good seasons at Gillingham and a final League campaign with Peterborough United. He gained coaching badges and returned to Roots Hall as youth development officer, before taking a similar position with Leyton Orient, a post he still holds.

Terry Johnson
Striker

Born: Newcastle-upon-Tyne, 30/8/1949

Joined: January 1971, from Newcastle

First team debut: v. York, 29/1/71

Appearances: 167(2)

Goals: 38

Other clubs: Longbenton, 1966-67; Newcastle, 1967-69; Brentford, 1974-76; Blyth Spartans, 1977-81

Terry signed as a professional for Newcastle United at the age of seventeen. He spent three seasons there, scoring 34 goals in his first season with the juniors, before moving up to the Central League side. During the 1968/69 season, he was top scorer with 15 goals, but he found it impossible to break into the first team. In November 1969, Terry scored a single goal in 4 loan appearances at Darlington, but when Arthur Rowley approached him to move to Roots Hall, he jumped at the chance. Terry came down on a Thursday and made his Blues debut the following day, scoring a great goal to give his new team a 1-0 win over York City.

Terry's 13 goals in the following campaign, his first full season at Southend, provided just the support Bill Garner and Billy Best needed, and the Blues were promoted to the Third Division. Terry's jinking wing play and excellent striking saw him become a firm fixture in the Blues team for the following campaign, but, after only 11 appearances in the 1974/75 season, it was clear that he could no longer rely on a regular first-team place, and he left the Blues to join Brentford in November 1974. Terry's goals-per-game ratio at Brentford was even better than at Southend, and he ended his League career with 63 goals from 262 appearances.

However, unlike most players, his disappearance from the League did not spell the end for Terry and his football career. He joined non-League Blyth Spartans, who were well-known at that time as being one of the giant-killing teams to avoid in the FA Cup draw. In the 1977/78 season, they made it to the fourth round to be rewarded with an away tie against Second Division Stoke City. In front of 18,000 fans, Terry scored in the first half to give the non-Leaguers the lead. Two goals in the second half put Stoke in front, but Blyth equalized in the 80th minute and, with only seconds remaining, Terry Johnson latched onto a Ron Guthrie free-kick to smash home the winner.

Blyth had become only the third non-League club in half a century to get to the fifth round. They duly went to the Racecourse Ground to face Wrexham and, with only two minutes left, were leading by another Terry Johnson goal. However, Dixie McNeill equalized, taking the tie to a replay, which was switched to St James's Park, Newcastle, allowing 42,157 to witness the game. Unfortunately, there was to be no fairy-tale this time, with Wrexham scoring twice in the first half. Although Terry pulled a goal back for Blyth in the second, it wasn't enough and the gallant non-Leaguers went out. Although he never played at St James's Park for Newcastle United, Terry finally got his chance and will always have the memory of scoring at his 'home' ground – even if it was for Blyth Spartans.

Emlyn 'Mickey' Jones
Striker

Born: Merthyr Tydfil, Dyfed, 29/11/1907

Joined: July 1929, from Everton

First team debut: v. Newport County, 31/8/29

Appearances: 236

Goals: 30

Other clubs: Merthyr Town, 1927-28; Bournemouth, 1928; Everton, 1928-29; Shirley Town, 1936-38; Barrow, 1938-39

Emlyn 'Mickey' Jones holds a unique record in Southend United history as he is the only Blues player to score for the club at Wembley Stadium. This is not a trick statement, despite the club never having reached a cup final of any sort. Southend played a League fixture against Clapton Orient – that they lost 1-3 – at Wembley (known then as the Empire Stadium) in December 1930, when Orient's Lea Bridge Road ground had been closed due to safety concerns. Orient were forced to hire the national stadium to stage two League fixtures while repairs were carried out at their own ground.

Jones had started his playing career with Merthyr Town, who were then a League side. He broke into the first team during the 1927/28 campaign, but the side struggled and had to apply for re-election. Jones then moved to Bournemouth, followed by Everton. Although he did not figure in the first team at Goodison Park, he starred for the reserves and learned much from training with the likes of Arthur Dominy, Eddie Critchley and Dixie Dean.

Jones joined Southend in July 1929. He became a favourite with manager Ted Birnie, as well as the Kursaal crowd. He slotted in at outside right and his industry and ability set up many goalscoring opportunities for the likes of Jimmy Shankly, Fred Baron and Dickie Donoven. Jones himself contributed 7 goals in

his first campaign and played in every match. The 1930/31 season saw him again play every match, scoring 8 goals. He was ever present again the following season and inspired Southend to their highest-ever placing of third in the Third Division (South), only four points behind champions Fulham.

Jones suffered a rare injury in the game against Bristol Rovers in August 1932, which ended a run of 133 consecutive appearances since joining the club from Everton. He remained a regular for Southend until Ted Birnie's departure in May 1934. Southend struggled in David Jack's first season in charge, eventually having to apply for re-election to the League, with Jack using thirty players during the 1934/35 season in an attempt to find a successful combination. Jones was to figure in only 23 League matches. The following season saw Jack sign a new outside right, Joe Firth from Leeds United, and Jones only appeared once in the entire campaign.

In 1936, Jones was allowed to leave after 236 appearances for Southend. He joined Shirley Town, who were playing in the high-profile Birmingham Combination. However, his League days were not over and he made 3 appearances for Barrow during 1938/39, the final season before the outbreak of war. Mickey Jones was at Roots Hall when his son, Ken, made his Southend United debut in December 1960.

Bobby Kellard

Striker

Born: Edmonton, North London, 1/3/1943

Joined: May 1960, from juniors

First team debut: v. Bradford, 29/9/59

Appearances: 113

Goals: 17

Other clubs: Crystal Palace, 1963-65 & 1971-72; Ipswich, 1965-66; Portsmouth, 1966-68 & 1972-74; Bristol City, 1968-70; Leicester, 1970-71; Torquay Utd

Born in 1943, Bobby came through the junior ranks at Southend United after attending Fairfax High School and made his debut on 29 September 1959 against Bradford City at Valley Parade, aged just 16 years and 208 days. He made himself a semi-permanent figure in the team for both this season and the following one. His accurate crosses and dazzling wing play would create many chances for the likes of Roy Hollis, Bud Houghton, Duggie Price and Sammy McCrory. During his Roots Hall career, much-travelled Blues striker Jim Fryatt described the youngster as one of the best prospects in the country.

In the 1960/61 season, both Peter Corthine and Fryatt scored more regularly when Kellard was in the side. He was an ever-present at number eleven during the 1961/62 season, when he scored 11 goals – only two less than top scorer Ken Jones. England youth honours, and a trial for the Great Britain Olympic team, were forthcoming whilst Bobby played for The Blues, but in 1963 he moved to Selhurst Park to join Crystal Palace for £9,500. Kellard made 77 appearances for The Eagles in just over two years and it was to prove the beginning of a nomadic career for Bobby, whose longest spell at any club was the three-and-a-quarter years he was with Southend.

A four-month spell at Portman Road with Ipswich was followed by a move to the south coast with Portsmouth, for whom he made nearly 100 League appearances. Two years and 77 appearances with The Robins of Bristol City was followed by a spell in the Midlands with Leicester City, who paid £50,000 for his services. Here, Bobby was a key figure in the side that finished as Second Division champions in 1970/71, making 40 appearances and scoring 7 goals in the season.

However, after only nine First Division appearances the following season, which included the winning goal in his final game – coincidentally against his previous club, Ipswich Town – Bobby was off on his travels again, this time returning to Crystal Palace. Palace's manager, Bert Head, paid out £55,000 for Kellard's services, but by December 1972, Bobby returned to another of his previous clubs, rejoining Portsmouth. Whilst at Fratton Park he had a brief loan spell at Hereford United, before spending some time playing in South Africa.

A two-match return to the English League with Torquay United in September 1975 brought the curtain down on a colourful career that spanned over 500 League appearances and over 50 goals. Although never reaching the heights of his Essex schoolboy team-mate Terry Venables, Bobby Kellard will always be remembered as a mercurial midfielder who gave his all for the many teams he played for.

Harry Lane
Striker

Born: Hednesford, Staffordshire, 21/3/1909

Joined: May 1933, from Birmingham*

First team debut: v. Crystal Palace, 26/8/33

Appearances: 245

Goals: 75

Other clubs: Hednesford, 1926-27; Bloxwich Strollers, 1927-29; Birmingham, 1930-31; Plymouth Argyle, 1938-39

Harry Lane's career started with his local team, Hednesford Town, who were playing in the Birmingham & District League (now known as the West Midlands League). After a season, he moved to Bloxwich Strollers, who competed in the Birmingham Combination. His prolific form there drew the attention of several League clubs in the area, but the Birmingham manager, Leslie Knighton, won the race for his signature in the summer of 1930.

Although Lane was to figure in only two first-team games at St Andrews, he was outstanding for the reserves. In May 1933, Southend manager Ted Birnie offered Lane the opportunity of regular first-team football. He accepted and his first season at Southend was the club's last at the old Kursaal ground. It was also to be Birnie's final season at the helm as The Blues struggled in the lower reaches of Division Three (South) all season. Lane contributed 9 goals and proved an excellent foil for the prolific Leo Stevens. In the 1934/35 season, Lane was played in a variety of forward positions as new manager David Jack struggled to choose his best attacking combination. However, the constant changes disrupted the team and the club were forced to apply for re-election after finishing next to bottom, six points ahead of Newport County.

The 1935/36 season saw more stability, although the team still struggled in the League,

and Lane top scored with 12 League goals. He also played in the epic FA Cup tie against Tottenham at White Hart Lane and scored the last goal in the dramatic 4-4 draw. This season also saw Lane's first hat-trick in a Blues shirt, when he hit three against Milwall. In February he got another hat-trick as Cardiff were thrashed 8-1. A month later, Lane scored yet another hat-trick in the 3-2 victory over QPR.

The 1937/38 season was to be his last during his first spell at the club when he lost his place to Robert Oswald and left for Plymouth in March 1938. He spent one full season at Home Park before the outbreak of war. Lane took part in some wartime football for Argyle and was a guest player for many other clubs, most notably for Nottingham Forest and Northampton.

When football resumed in 1946, Harry Lane, despite being thirty-seven, was re-engaged for Southend by Harry Warren and proved his worth by scoring twice in his first game back. His experience benefited local youngsters Cyril Thompson and Frank Dudley, as the trio hit 59 goals between them, Lane's contribution being 16. The following season he was used less regularly and played his last game for Southend in January 1949, two months before his fortieth birthday. Harry Lane was a tremendous servant to the club either side of the war and a reliable goalscorer throughout his career.

Mike Lapper
Defender

Born: Redondo Beach, USA, 28/8/1970

Joined: July 1995, from US Soccer Federation

First team debut: v. Portsmouth, 12/8/95

Appearances: 53(6)

Goals: 1

Other clubs: US Soccer Federation, 1991-94; VfL Wolfsburg (Germany), 1994-95; Columbus Crew (USA), 1997-present

Mike Lapper was born in California in 1970 and was a member of UCLA's 1990 NCAA Division One championship-winning team, before being selected for the All-America first team in 1991. He made his international debut for the United States in April 1991, against South Korea in Pohang, and was an ever present in the national side that participated in the 1992 Olympic Games in Spain. From January 1993, many US internationals were contracted exclusively to the United States Soccer Federation in preparation for their hosting of the 1994 World Cup finals. Instead of being sidetracked by club matches, they solely played international fixtures and Lapper soon clocked up 44 caps. Lapper was selected for the 1994 World Cup squad, but lost his place in the starting eleven at the last minute to the emerging Alexi Lalas.

After the World Cup, Lapper moved to German Second Division outfit VfL Wolfsburg, for whom he scored on his debut. At the end of the 1994/95 season, he briefly returned to the US before joining Southend United in July 1995. He made his debut in the opening game of the 1995/96 season, a 2-4 defeat at Portsmouth. A tall and commanding centre-back, Mike soon became a favourite at Roots Hall with his brash, no-nonsense approach to defending. His Southend career was put on hold

after breaking his leg during a 1-0 Boxing Day victory over Norwich City. It was to cost him the remainder of that campaign.

He had a less spectacular season during 1996/97 and, after a dispute over alleged unpaid transfer fees with the USSF, Lapper returned to the States in the summer of 1997. The newly instigated Major League Soccer was recruiting players and Lapper joined Columbus Crew, whom he led to the play-offs whilst making 20 appearances and scoring a goal. Unfortunately, the 1998 season was another curtailed by injury, with a torn Achilles tendon restricting Mike to only 7 games.

The 1999 campaign proved to be much better, with Lapper making 31 appearances having fully recovered from surgery to repair his troublesome Achilles. Mike was a popular and active member of the church community whilst in the Southend area, always giving to those he felt were less fortunate than himself. On his return to America, he gave his car to the church so they could sell it to raise funds. As a Blues player, he will probably be best remembered for his quirky, off-the-wall column, 'Lapper's Patter' in the local paper. He also left his mark on life at Roots Hall, being the first player to wear flip-flops during leisure time to reduce wear and tear on the feet – a practice that has been adopted by several Blues players since.

Micky Laverick
Midfielder

Born: Trimdon, Co. Durham, 13/3/1954

Joined: October 1976, from Mansfield

First team debut: v. Exeter, 23/10/76

Appearances: 125(2)

Goals: 19

Other clubs: Mansfield, 1972-75; Huddersfield, 1979-81; York, 1982-83

Micky Laverick was spotted playing for Ollerton Youth Club and eventually signed professional forms with Mansfield Town in January 1972, after serving his apprenticeship at Field Mill. An industrious midfielder, he won the Notts Senior Cup with Mansfield in 1972 before he made his first-team debut in the opening game of the 1972/73 season. Mansfield set the Fourth Division alight early on, with Micky playing a starring role. However, the season turned sour after Christmas for both Laverick and the Stags, a slump in form leaving Town in sixth place and Micky out of the first-team picture.

After a poor 1973/74 season, in which Micky made 36 appearances, Mansfield again stormed the Fourth Division, this time finishing as champions by six points. Unfortunately, Micky could only muster 11 appearances, but the 1975/76 season saw Micky at his best. With Mansfield languishing in bottom position and having sacked Dave Smith, Micky commanded the midfield for the final 15 matches of the season for which the club remained unbeaten. He claimed three goals and led the club to the safety of eleventh place in the table.

In October 1976, Southend manager Dave Smith returned to Field Mill to bring Micky Laverick to Roots Hall and, although not an immediate hit with the Southend fans, his midfield endeavours won them over. Micky went on to make 34 appearances, scoring 4 times, in his first campaign for the Blues. The 1977/78 season proved to be the pinnacle of his Southend career, as he missed only one match, with Southend finishing as runners-up in the Fourth Division. He also ended the season as the club's third top scorer. Laverick followed this with 6 goals in the 1978/79 season.

The 1979/80 season saw Micky move to Huddersfield Town, and he proved an immediate hit at Leeds Road. He missed only one game as the Terriers won the Fourth Division title, but after half a season in the Third Division in 1980/81, Micky dropped out of favour, and was eventually sold to York City in January 1982. After only 5 wins in their opening 25 League matches, Micky's midfield skills helped them to nine wins in the latter part of the season, saving the club from the ignominy of having to apply for re-election. He was unable to retain his place in the team for 1982/83 and was loaned to Huddersfield.

This was to be the end of Laverick's successful League career, although he later played non-League football for Boston United and Ollerton. When his playing days were over, Micky avoided the obvious route of becoming a manager, opting instead to become a prison officer in Nottinghamshire.

Jimmy Lawler
Striker/Defender

Born: Dublin, 20/11/1923

Joined: January 1949, from Portsmouth

First team debut: v. Port Vale, 22/1/49

Appearances: 288

Goals: 17

Other clubs: Glentoran, 1941-47; Portsmouth, 1947-49; Chelmsford, 1957-59

Although Jimmy Lawler was born in Dublin, it was to be in Northern Ireland that he made his name as a quick and skilful inside forward with Glentoran. He progressed to the first team and, although the Irish League had been suspended due to the war, competed in the Irish Cup, which was still being contested, sadly losing in the final on three occasions.

Lawler was keen to try his skills in the English League and secured a move to Portsmouth in the summer of 1947. He spent two seasons at Fratton Park and, although overlooked for first-team duties, Lawler excelled in Football Combination matches. In January 1949, Southend manager Harry Warren was looking to strengthen his squad and took a look at Lawler. Warren was impressed with the Irishman and signed him at once, with Lawler slotting into the forward line alongside Frank Dudley, Cyril Grant and Tommy Tippett.

After eighteen months at the club, Lawler was struggling to hold a regular place in the side, but Warren had the brainwave of trying him at half-back. Despite his lack of height – he was 5' 8" – the conversion was a resounding success, Lawler's pace making up for his lack of inches. He fitted in with Jackie French and Jimmy Stirling in a formidable half-back line. Lawler was ever present during the 1951/52 season, with French missing only one game and Frank Sheard

and Stirling battling for the single remaining half-back slot.

In February 1953, Lawler scored in a game at Aldershot, but late in the second half sustained a knee injury that would halt his run of 99 consecutive appearances in the Southend side. He returned briefly but, unfortunately, he suffered a reoccurrence of the injury at Carrow Road and this time he was out of the side for 9 matches. In the 1953/54 season, he suffered a string of injuries which would restrict him to only a dozen games, during which time new signings Bill Pavitt and Jim Duthie established themselves in the team. Lawler regained full fitness in September 1954 and formed a new half-back line with Frank Burns and Denis Howe.

In April 1955, the club rewarded Lawler's consistency with a benefit match against his former club, Portsmouth. Lawler was again a regular during the 1955/56 season, missing only 4 matches in a memorable campaign. The first season at the newly opened Roots Hall saw the Blues finish fourth in the Third Division (South) and also reach the fourth round of the FA Cup. Lawler finally lost his place in the Southend side in March 1957, when the promising John Duffy came into the team. He retired from the professional game at the end of that campaign, but wound down a fine career with a couple of seasons with Southern League Chelmsford City.

Mike Marsh
Midfielder

Born: Liverpool

Joined: August 1995, from Galatasaray

First team debut: v. Sunderland, 9/9/95

Appearances: 97

Goals: 13

Other clubs: Kirkby, 1985-87; Liverpool, 1987-93; West Ham, 1993-94; Coventry, 1994-95; Galatasaray (Turkey), 1995; Barrow, 1997-98; Southport, 1998-99 & 2000-01; Kidderminster Harriers, 1999-2000

Strangely, considering his undoubted talent, Mike Marsh slipped through the nets of all three Merseyside clubs as a youngster. Instead, he worked his way up to the professional game from non-League football. He came to the attention of Liverpool having starred for the now defunct Kirkby Town, who were playing in the North West Counties League.

It was Liverpool manager Kenny Dalglish who finally brought him to Anfield in August 1987. Marsh had to wait until March 1989 for his first-team debut as a substitute for Jan Molby in a 2-0 victory over Charlton. Perhaps it was unsurprising that Marsh initially struggled to make an impact, as Liverpool's midfield included the likes of Ronnie Whelan, Ray Houghton, Steve McMahon, John Barnes and Jan Molby. The next two seasons continued to be a testing time, with Marsh making only 4 League appearances for The Reds. However, the 1991/92 campaign saw him really make the breakthrough, playing the majority of League matches and picking up an FA Cup winners' medal – Marsh was a non-playing substitute as Liverpool defeated Sunderland 2-0 at Wembley.

He continued to feature for The Reds during the 1992/93 campaign and scored three penalties during Liverpool's Coca-Cola Cup run that ended in defeat at Crystal Palace. In September 1993, Marsh moved to West Ham for £400,000 and although he became a popular figure at Upton Park, his family failed to settle in the south and by December 1994 he was on the move again. This time Marsh signed for Coventry, with £450,000 changing hands. His stay at Highfield Road was less than successful and by the summer of 1995 he accepted Graeme Souness' offer to join him in Turkey, where the former Liverpool legend had taken over as coach of Galatasaray. Souness had already signed another former Liverpool colleague, Barry Venison, and saw Marsh as his midfield playmaker.

After only three matches in Istanbul, Marsh and his family were desperately homesick and when Southend player/manager Ronnie Whelan needed a new midfielder, the Turkish side were glad to recoup their £500,000 investment. The price was a Southend record transfer fee and Whelan, who knew Marsh's ability well from their Anfield days, was put in the strange position of replacing himself in the team after his own playing career was ended by a knee injury. Marsh was in a very similar mould to Whelan – hard-working, technically

gifted and capable of changing a game with a defence-splitting pass. His presence in the side guided Southend to mid-table respectability in Division One.

The 1996/97 season was to prove a disaster for Marsh and The Blues. In a match against Reading in November he sustained knee ligament and cartilage damage. While he was out of the side, Southend slumped to such a bad position that relegation could not be avoided when he reclaimed his place. Whelan departed in the summer and Marsh was soon at odds with new incumbent, Alvin Martin. However, a clash of personalities did not end Marsh's Roots Hall career – instead it was a clash of bodies in a match against Bristol City in October 1997, which saw Marsh suffer severe cruciate ligament damage, and, combined with the previous knee injury, Marsh's professional career was over.

He accepted an insurance payout of £400,000, but could not keep out of the game for long. He took on the coach's position at non-League Barrow, which was followed by a similar stint at Southport. A couple of seasons away from the playing side did wonders for his knee problem and, in the summer of 1998, he joined Kidderminster Harriers after impressing their manager, and former Liverpool teammate, Jan Molby.

With Marsh's drive and ability in the middle of the park, Harriers stormed to the Conference championship and thus elevation to the Football League. Marsh's remarkable comeback was crowned when he was voted Conference Player of the Year. However, due to clauses in his insurance payout agreement, Marsh was unable to join Kidderminster in the Football League. Instead, he linked up with yet another former Liverpool colleague, Mark Wright, at Southport. Mike Marsh was undoubtedly a prodigious talent and his value to The Blues was most apparent when he was missing from the side; in his absence, Southend would invariably be outclassed in midfield. In October 2001 he retired again, after a brief spell with Boston United.

Dave Martin
Utility

Born: East Ham, London, 25/4/1963

Joined: August 1986, from Wimbledon

First team debut: v. Peterborough, 23/8/86

Appearances: 256(11)

Goals: 28

Other clubs: Millwall, 1979-84; Wimbledon, 1984-85; Bristol City, 1993-94; Gillingham, 1995-96; Leyton Orient, 1996-97; Northampton, 1997

Dave Martin was part of the Millwall youth team that won the FA Youth Cup. After winning England youth caps, Millwall offered him professional terms in May 1980. He already had first-team experience, having made his Lions debut at the age of sixteen, in March 1980. After making 140 League appearances in four-and-a-half years at The Den, Wimbledon signed him, and he made his Dons debut as a substitute in September 1984. Martin flitted in and out of the first team during his first season at Plough Lane, and it was little different in his second season, when The Dons gained promotion to the First Division.

Just 15 League matches and a single goal in the 1985/86 season signalled an end to his Wimbledon career, and Martin signed for the Blues in August 1986. Being such a versatile player, Martin found himself utilized as a full-back, centre half, midfielder and even centre forward during a seven-year spell at Roots Hall. He made 39 appearances and contributed 5 goals in a season that saw Southend gain promotion to the Third Division.

The following campaign saw Martin in a mainly defensive role, and he ended the season having made more appearances than any other Blues player, but only managing a solitary goal from his 50 games. He settled into a central midfield role for the 1988/89 season, but the Blues were to suffer relegation. However, things improved in 1989/90, with a strong midfield helping drive the Shrimpers to promotion. It was the 1990/91 season that most Blues fans will remember him for, as his support from midfield brought him a remarkable tally of 14 goals from 48 matches as Southend finished runners-up in the Third Division. A triumphant season saw five Blues players reach double-figure goal tallies.

Sadly, Martin was injured just five games into the 1991/92 campaign. He played no further part in the season for Southend, though he helped out his former team-mate, Roy McDonough, who was then player-manager of non-League Colchester United. Martin was loaned to the U's for the last two months of the season and helped guide Colchester to the Conference and FA Trophy double.

He returned to Roots Hall with a bang, scoring in the 1992/93 campaign opener at St James' Park against Newcastle, but he never truly recovered his form and at the end of the season was transferred to Bristol City. He never shone for the Robins and, following a loan spell at Northampton in February 1995, he signed for Gillingham. His League career ended with brief stints at Leyton Orient, Northampton and Brighton. Dave Martin currently owns a greetings card store in Upminster.

Jimmy McAlinden
Midfielder

Born: Belfast, 13/12/1917

Died: Belfast, 18/1/1994

Joined: October 1948, from Stoke

First team debut: v. Watford, 16/10/48

Appearances: 231

Goals: 13

Other clubs: Belfast Celtic, 1935-38 & 1940-44; Portsmouth, 1938-40 & 1946-47; Shamrock Rovers, 1945-46; Stoke, 1947-48

Born in Belfast in 1917, Jimmy McAlinden was raised within the shadow of Belfast Celtic's legendary Paradise Ground. He was a keen follower of the side as a youngster and was overjoyed to be signed by Celtic's new manager, Elisha Scott, in 1934 as a sixteen-year-old. The young McAlinden had impressed the former Liverpool player when starring for Glentoran Seconds against Celtic Seconds. He was out of work at the time and was taken on as a full-time professional, training four mornings a week and being paid the princely sum of £2 a week. The youngster's blistering pace and midfield scheming became the fulcrum of an all-conquering Celtic side that would eventually take five successive Irish League titles from 1935 to 1940. Jimmy McAlinden missed out on the Irish Cup final of 1937 due to injury, but scored in the final twelve months later, when The Celts defeated Bangor 2-1 to raise the trophy.

By 1938, McAlinden, now twenty-one, made no secret of his desire to move to England. Tottenham and Huddersfield both expressed an interest in him after he had shown his calibre in two international matches for Ireland against Scotland in 1937 and 1938. However, it was Portsmouth who won the race for his signature, paying £7,500 for his services in December 1938. Within six months of arriving at Fratton Park, McAlinden had yet another winners' medal as Pompey defeated Wolves 4-1 in the FA Cup final of 1939. His burgeoning career was halted by the outbreak of the Second World War and, finding his contract cancelled, McAlinden returned to Belfast Celtic.

He spent the 1945/46 season with Shamrock Rovers, returning to Portsmouth when Football League action resumed in 1946. In June 1947 he joined Stoke City, before the Southend manager, Harry Warren, parted with a then club record fee of £6,500 to bring him to Essex in October 1948. The Ulsterman became the driving force and captain of the excellent Blues post-war side, who were capable of scintillating football – which would usually be inspired by the mercurial midfield play of 'Jimmy Mac'. His form was so good with Southend that he was recalled to the Irish national side, winning his fourth and final international cap against England in October 1948.

In May 1950, it came to the attention of the Football Association that McAlinden had accepted a £750 signing-on fee from

Portsmouth manager Jack Tinn, a practice that was illegal at the time. Although the offence had occured some twelve years earlier, Southend United suffered the brunt of the FA's wrath, with McAlinden being fined a hefty £50 and banned for an amazing four months. For an offence committed by another club, Southend were forced to play without their guiding light for the first twelve matches of the 1950/51 season. Despite the lengthy ban, McAlinden went on to clock up 231 appearances for The Blues, before retiring from the full-time game in July 1954 at the age of thirty-six.

His final match for Southend, against QPR in April 1954, saw him leave the pitch at the Southend Stadium to a spontaneous and heartfelt standing ovation from a crowd of 10,000. McAlinden took up an offer of the player-manager position at Glentoran. In the 1956/57 season he guided Glentoran to the Irish League and Cup double. He later managed Distillery and Drogheda. Jimmy McAlinden died in 1994, aged seventy-six.

Sam McCrory

Striker

Born: Belfast, 11/10/1924

Joined: June 1955, from Plymouth Argyle

First team debut: v. Norwich, 20/8/55

Appearances: 222

Goals: 99

Other clubs: Linfield (N. Ireland), 1942-46; Swansea, 1946-49; Ipswich, 1949-51; Plymouth Argyle, 1952-54

Sam McCrory started his career with Linfield in his native Belfast, playing wartime matches while the Northern Ireland League was suspended during the hostilities. He moved to Swansea Town for the 1946/47 season, when normal football activities resumed. Despite suffering relegation to the Third Division (South) in his first season at the Vetch Field, he had a highly successful time in Wales, culminating in a Third Division (South) championship medal in 1948/49, when McCrory contributed 20 of The Swans' 87 goals in a memorable campaign.

In March 1950, Ipswich manager, Scott Duncan, parted with £18,000 to bring McCrory and his Swansea team mate, Jim Feeney, to Portman Road. He scored regularly for Ipswich, but in the summer of 1952 moved to Plymouth. Having gained promotion to the Second Division, the Argyle manager, Jimmy Rae, needed to strengthen his forward line and McCrory fitted the bill. In his first season at Home Park, Argyle finished in a highly creditable fourth place. In the summer of 1955, Jack Rowley replaced Rae as manager of Plymouth and the thirty-year-old McCrory

was, surprisingly, allowed to leave Home Park for a bargain £1,000 fee. He joined Southend, who had moved back to Roots Hall for the start of the 1955/56 campaign, and McCrory had the honour of scoring the first goal at the new ground when The Blues defeated Norwich 3-1.

He played every match in his first season, contributing 19 goals to finish second to Roy Hollis in the scoring chart. The 1956/57 campaign was particularly memorable for McCrory, as he scored his first Blues hat-trick in a 4-1 FA Cup demolition of Colchester at Layer Road. In 1957/58, with McCrory now approaching the veteran age of thirty-three, he had his finest season at Roots Hall, becoming only the second Southend player to score 30 League goals in a season – following Jimmy Shankly's 34 goals in 1928/29. His haul included three hat-tricks, against Walsall, Port Vale and Northampton. His exceptional form belatedly earned him international recognition. In October 1957, McCrory was picked to play in Northern Ireland's first ever 'B' international, against Rumania, at Windsor Park. McCrory opened the scoring in a 6-0 victory. The following month, McCrory made his full debut against England at Wembley. He had a sensational game, running the show and scoring in a 3-2 win, Ireland's first victory against

England for thirty years. His performance won rave reviews, but despite being picked for the World Cup squad in Sweden in 1958, it was to be his only international appearance.

The 1958/59 season saw McCrory play all but two games, although he lost his top scorer's crown to newcomer Bud Houghton. His final campaign at Roots Hall, 1959/60, saw stiff competition from Roy Hollis, Duggie Price and Houghton and when Eddie Perry signed Peter Corthine from Chelsea, McCrory realised his opportunities were going to be restricted.

Fittingly, he scored in his last appearance in a Blues shirt at York in April 1960, taking his goal tally for Southend to 99. McCrory spent a season with Cambridge United, who were then in the Southern League, but in the summer of 1961 he was offered a player-manager role at Crusaders in his home city. His stint in charge at Seaview, however, was brief and McCrory later ran a Belfast pub for many years. Sam McCrory was not only one of Southend's greatest goalscorers, but remains the only Blues player ever to score a goal at international level.

Roy McDonough
Striker

Born: Solihull, West Midlands, 16/10/1958

Joined: August 1983, from Colchester Utd*

First team debut: v. Rotherham, 27/8/83

Appearances: 216(26)

Goals: 40

Other clubs: Birmingham, 1976-78; Walsall, 1978-80; Chelsea, 1980-81; Colchester, 1981-83 & 1990-94; Exeter, 1983-84; Cambridge, 1984-85

Roy McDonough holds a unique place in football history. His career total of thirteen red cards is a Football League record that even exceeds the efforts of players like Vinnie Jones and Julian Dicks. 'Rebel', 'renegade' and 'maverick' are all suitable adjectives for the Solihull-born forward who began his career as a schoolboy at Aston Villa.

He was rejected by Villa Park but went on to gain an apprenticeship and play professionally for Birmingham City in October 1974, making his first-team debut in May 1977. Despite scoring on his second appearance, he could not break the regular strike partnership of Trevor Francis and John Connolly. He was sold to Walsall in September 1978 and had a successful 1979/80 campaign, helping The Saddlers gain promotion from the Fourth Division. He only scored 7 goals himself but set up many for others.

Chelsea manager, Geoff Hurst signed him in October 1980. However, he was never picked for the first-team and was sold on to Colchester United only four months later. In August 1983, McDonough arrived at Roots Hall, although his first spell with The Blues was to prove inauspicious. Southend were struggling under new manager Peter Morris and the new signing managed only 4 goals in 26 games.

By January 1984, McDonough had lost his place to Trevor Whymark and was released to join Exeter City on a free transfer, which was followed by a spell with Cambridge United. In the summer of 1985, Bobby Moore re-signed the tall striker for Southend. In his second spell he showed better form, although Shrimpers fans were divided in their opinion of him. His hard-hitting tackles and quick temper often saw him in trouble with referees. In his first season back at Roots Hall, an FA Cup tie with Newport County was only six minutes old when McDonough received his marching orders.

In front of goal, his best season for the Blues was 1987/88, when he scored 11 times in 50 games. His Roots Hall career ended in May 1990, when he rejoined Colchester United who had just been relegated to the Conference. He took over as player-manager in August 1991 and guided The U's to the Conference and FA Trophy double as they regained their Football League status after only two seasons. His League career ended when he was sacked by the Colchester chairman – who was also his father-in-law – at the end of the 1993/94 campaign.

McDonough then played for a host of local non-League clubs, including Chelmsford City, Braintree Town and Heybridge Swifts. A hot-headed, but lovable rogue with an excellent work-rate, McDonough will be best remembered for his perpetual look of innocence when confronted by yet another card-brandishing official.

John McGuigan
Striker

Born: Motherwell, Strathclyde, 29/10/1932

Joined: May 1955, from St Mirren

First team debut: v. Norwich, 20/8/55

Appearances: 138

Goals: 36

Other clubs: St Mirren, 1952-55; Newcastle, 1958-62; Scunthorpe, 1962-63; Southampton, 1963-64; Swansea Town, 1964-65

Born in Motherwell, John McGuigan came to the fore with St Mirren, where he became a highly-rated outside left. After three seasons, McGuigan wanted to try his luck in the English League and joined The Blues in May 1955, after Southend manager Harry Warren had received glowing recommendations.

His first season was the club's first at the newly-built Roots Hall and it saw McGuigan feature in every match of the campaign, alongside team mates Jim Duthie and Sammy McCrory. In what was to prove to be Warren's last season in charge of The Blues, the club enjoyed a memorable campaign, finishing fourth in the Third Division (South) and losing narrowly in the FA Cup fourth round to a great Manchester City side – who would win the coveted trophy that year. Southend scored an amazing 93 League and cup goals, with McGuigan helping himself to 13 – a figure that left him trailing in the wake of Roy Hollis (26), Sam McCrory (19) and Kevin Baron (15).

The 1956/57 season saw McGuigan again featuring prominently, although niggling injuries saw him miss five matches when his fellow countryman, Alex Duchart, deputised. McGuigan's third and final season at the club, 1957/58, again saw Southend scoring freely – this time a tally of 98 in all competitions was achieved. McGuigan contributed 12 goals, but

his skilful play and undoubted ability set up many chances for McCrory and Hollis. It was apparent that McGuigan was more than capable of playing at a higher level and it was no real surprise when he joined First Division Newcastle in July 1958 for a tidy fee of £8,000. He progressed well at St James Park under the 'Bogota Bandit' Charlie Mitten. However, Newcastle struggled in the League and Mitten was eventually sacked in October 1961, being replaced by Norman Smith.

Smith brought in many new players and, in January 1962, McGuigan found himself a victim of the reshuffle when he was sold to Scunthorpe United. He had a successful spell at the Old Show Ground, with The Irons finishing ninth in the Second Division in his only full season with the club. In the summer of 1963, he was sold to Southampton and, as with many of his transfers, McGuigan's arrival resulted in improved fortunes as The Saints finished fifth in the Second Division. McGuigan's final move came in March 1965 when he joined Swansea Town. However, this time his arrival at the Vetch Field came too late to stop The Swans getting relegated to the Third Division.

McGuigan retired from the game in 1966 at the age of thirty-four. He will be remembered as an integral part of a Blues line-up that seemed to be able to score goals at will.

John McKinven
Striker

Born: Campbelltown, Strathclyde, 1/5/1941

Joined: May 1960, from Raith Rovers

First team debut: v. Shrewsbury, 26/9/60

Appearances: 303(3)

Goals: 66

Other clubs: Raith Rovers, 1958-60; Cambridge Utd, 1969-70

A talented outside left, John McKinven started his career in 1958 with Raith Rovers, who played in the Scottish First Division. After a couple of seasons at Stark's Park, McKinven joined Southend on a free transfer in May 1960.

His first season at Roots Hall saw Frank Broome's squad overloaded with forward players, but McKinven made his debut against Shrewsbury in September 1960 and opened his scoring account in the next match at Brentford. He played in about half the games that season and the majority of matches in the following campaign, which saw Ted Fenton in charge of the Blues. The 1961/62 season was frustrating for McKinven and Southend, as Fenton constantly changed the team and tactics. His third season at the club saw a more settled Blues line-up finish a respectable eighth in the Third Division. McKinven scored 12 goals, including a fabulous hat-trick in a 3-2 win over Bristol Rovers.

The next two seasons saw McKinven playing virtually every match. One player to profit from McKinven's wing wizardry was Bobby Gilfillan, who arrived in June 1963. The 1964/65 campaign was prolific for both men, McKinven netting 11 goals and Gilfillan doubling that figure – with many of them coming from an uncanny ability to anticipate where McKinven's crosses were landing. McKinven was awarded a benefit match against a Select XI in April 1965. The

1965/66 campaign saw Southend with a new manager, Alvan Williams, and the season proved to be a disaster. The Blues were relegated for the first time in their history and McKinven played in the club's humiliating record defeat, 1-9 at Brighton, in November. His season was ended prematurely in March 1966 with an injury. This kept him out of the game until January 1967, when he regained his place at the expense of the impressive youngster, John Baber.

Despite such a long lay-off, McKinven's form recovered spectacularly for the 1967/68 season – Ernie Shepherd's first full campaign in charge, having been promoted from assistant manager following Williams' resignation. He missed only two League matches and was joint top scorer for the season on 17 goals. The next season was only a dozen games old when McKinven suffered a heavy tackle. Southend supporters in the East Stand heard a sickening crack as McKinven's leg was broken. He missed the remainder of the season and only appeared in three more matches for Southend. Even after moving to Cambridge United for the 1970/71 season, he never regained his form and retired from the game after Cambridge's first League season. The 1960s was a decade of struggle at Roots Hall, but McKinven had been a constant and much loved figure during this turbulent period in Southend's history.

Keith Mercer
Striker

Born: Lewisham, South London, 14/10/1956

Joined: February 1980, from Watford

First team debut: v. Millwall, 12/2/80

Appearances: 151

Goals: 36

Other clubs: Watford, 1972-79; Blackpool, 1983-84

Keith Mercer was an unlikely looking footballer, but his close control and ball skills saw him enjoy a highly successful, if brief, career. He signed as an apprentice with Watford and progressed through the ranks until he was awarded a first-team debut in February 1973. The Hornets started the 1973/74 season with a new manager, Mike Keen, who totally ignored the young Mercer. However, he started making progress during the 1974/75 campaign, making 15 League appearances and scoring his first senior goal. He really came to the fore during 1975/76, when he would often come off the substitutes bench to score vital goals. He made 23 appearances (11 as a sub), but he still managed an excellent tally of 10 goals – including his first hat-trick in a match against Exeter City.

However, the 1976/77 season saw the arrival of Graham Taylor and he implemented a 4-3-3 formation. Mercer and his two strike partners hit 46 goals between them, Mercer leading the way with 22. The following campaign was less prolific for him, but his 14 League and cup goals contributed to a highly successful season, which saw Watford lift the Fourth Division title. Although Watford gained a second successive promotion in 1978/79, Mercer lost his place to the emerging Luther Blissett. In February 1980, Southend manager, Dave Smith, saw Mercer as the missing piece for his new strike-force.

Although his arrival at Roots Hall could not prevent relegation, Mercer's worth was proven in the 1980/81 championship-winning side. He contributed 10 goals himself, but also provided many opportunities for Derek Spence and Terry Gray. The following campaign saw Mercer top score for the Blues with 13 League goals.

Mercer's last campaign at Roots Hall was interesting on a personal level, despite the club's mid-table position. He linked up well with Steve Phillips and scored 9 goals. His most memorable match, however, came in September 1982 in the game against Doncaster. Blues were leading 3-1 when goalkeeper John Keeley was sent off under the new professional foul rule and Mercer was forced to take over in goal. His first act was to pick the ball out of the net as Rovers' Steve Lister crashed the resulting free kick into the top corner. After that, he managed to save everything Doncaster could muster as Blues held on for a dramatic victory.

Mercer left Southend in 1983 and joined Blackpool. A promising season was cut short in March 1984, when he sustained serious knee ligament damage that would end his professional career at the age of twenty-eight. It was good to see that Mercer had lost none of his popularity among Southend supporters when he turned out for Ron Pountney's belated testimonial match in August 2000.

George Molyneux
Defender

Born: Liverpool, c. 1875

Died: Southend, 14/4/1942

Joined: June 1906, from Portsmouth

First team debut: v. Swindon Res, 1/9/1906

Appearances: 206

Goals: 2

Other clubs: Everton, 1897-98 & 1898-1900; Wigan County, 1898; Southampton, 1900-05; Portsmouth, 1905-06; Colchester Town, 1911-14

When Bob Jack was shaping the first-ever Southend United squad he knew he wanted a reliable and influential player to marshal his defence. He chose the former England international George Molyneux, who, despite being thirty-one years old, was to prove a pivotal player in Southend's formative years.

Molyneux had joined Everton in 1897, after serving in the army for several years, but was released after only one first-team game. He briefly turned out for South Shore, but then joined Wigan County, where he impressed sufficiently to earn a move back to Goodison in 1898. He was then a fairly regular member of The Toffees' first team, but opted for a move to Southampton in 1900. The Saints were a formidable side and took three Southern League championships during his five-year stay. In 1902, they reached the FA Cup final, but lost the replay, 2-1, after their initial 1-1 draw with Sheffield United.

Whilst at The Dell, Molyneux formed a good friendship with C.B. Fry – often described as England's greatest sportsman, having been a dual internationalist at football and cricket as well as holding the world long jump record! He followed Fry into the England team, making his debut against Scotland in May 1902. Tragically, Molyneux was to witness an horrific crowd disaster that day when 26 fans were killed and more

than 500 injured when a stand behind the goal collapsed. Molyneux went on to gain 4 caps for England.

In June 1905 he moved to Portsmouth and helped Pompey finished third in the Southern League. Molyneux then moved to Roots Hall in June 1906 and was appointed club captain, his physical presence garnering respect from team mates and opponents alike. During the close seasons, he was an efficient opening batsman for Leigh Cricket Club. When Bob Jack left in 1910, Molyneux was appointed his successor in a player-manager role. His six months in charge, however, were a disaster as Southend were relegated back to Southern League Division Two.

Molyneux remained a hero with supporters and they turned out in droves for his benefit match in 1911. He then moved to Colchester Town, and during the First World War played in the army's representative team. He lived in Southend for the remainder of his life, working as an engineer in Eastern Avenue. In 1942, Molyneux contracted cancer of the tongue and died at his home in North Road. It is a testament to the hardship faced by footballers in those times that this once great and respected player died in obscurity with only his sisters in attendance at his funeral. It is an honour to permanently record George Molyneux's contribution to the early history of Southend United.

Stan Montgomery
Defender/Midfielder

Born: West Ham, East London, 7/7/1920

Joined: September 1946, from Hull

First team debut: v. Leyton Orient, 19/9/46

Appearances: 100

Goals: 7

Other clubs: Romford, 1938-39; Hull, 1944-47; Cardiff, 1948-55; Worcester, 1955; Newport County, 1955-56

Stan Montgomery was a powerfully built right-half who could effortlessly switch to inside right when required. Montgomery joined Athenian League Romford as an eighteen-year-old but war broke out and Montgomery's fledgling career was put on hold. In 1944, he signed a contract with Hull City and played 10 games for them in the emergency League Championship North. Hull withdrew from wartime football for the 1945/46 season and Montgomery returned south to see his family. He played for Southend as a guest, competing in the confusingly titled Third Division South (North Region) and turned in some excellent performances at right-half.

When the League resumed for the 1946/47 season, Montgomery returned to Boothferry Park, but only briefly. After five matches of the new season Harry Warren persuaded Montgomery to sign for Southend on a permanent basis. He made his debut in a goal-less draw with Leyton Orient and soon formed a formidable half-back combination with Arthur Harris and Bob Jackson. The 1947/48 campaign saw him play in all but one of Southend's matches. In the 1948/49 season, Warren often used Montgomery in a forward position and he scored both goals in a 2-2 draw against Leyton Orient.

In November 1948, Montgomery joined Second Division Cardiff City. The Bluebirds

manager, Cyril Spiers, converted Montgomery from right half to centre half and he excelled in this new position. After finishing fourth and third, Cardiff finally won promotion to the First Division in 1951/52, when they were runners-up to Sheffield Wednesday. Montgomery was a rock during the three campaigns and would skipper the side in the absence of Cardiff legend Alf Sherwood. Montgomery, and Cardiff, adapted well to life in the top flight, finishing in a respectable mid-table position. He played a total of three First Division seasons for Cardiff before he was released from Ninian Park in the summer of 1955. It was no coincidence that, after his departure, The Bluebirds struggled and were relegated at the end of the 1956/57 campaign.

In July 1955, Montgomery joined Southern League Worcester City, but after only three months, he was summoned back to the League with Newport County. In October 1956 he was released and joined Llanelli, where he wound down his football career. However, football was not Montgomery's only talent. He also excelled at cricket and, whilst at Southend, played for Essex's Second Eleven in the Minor Counties League. In 1949, he signed for Glamorgan and played for the Welsh county for five consecutive summers. Montgomery was a tremendous athlete and a genuine member of that sadly long-lost football/cricket dual sportsman's club.

Alan Moody

Defender

Born: Middlesbrough, Cleveland, 18/1/1951

Joined: October 1972, from Middlesbrough

First team debut: v. Watford, 14/10/72

Appearances: 504(2)

Goals: 44

Other clubs: Middlesbrough, 1968-72; Maldon Town, 1984-85

Born in 1951, Alan used to cheer on his local team, Middlesbrough, with his father, watching the legendary goalscoring talent of Brian Clough. Although starting as a tenacious left-back, Alan soon converted to a centre half under the tutelage of next-door-neighbour Billy Day, who was a member of the same Middlesbrough team as Clough. Alan shone at athletics, cricket and basketball, but began to carve himself a reputation as a footballer, firstly being chosen to captain Middlesbrough schools, then being selected to play for Yorkshire. Eventually he was invited to join the England schoolboys squad, gaining a cap against Scotland at Ibrox – where he played at right-back and laid on England's equalizer in a 1-1 draw.

In 1966, Alan earned another international call, when the entire Middlesbrough schools team were called on to serve as ball boys in the World Cup finals. Alan was on duty at Wembley for the third place play-off and was behind the goal that Eusebio struck a penalty into past the great Russian goalkeeper, Lev Yashin. Alan became an apprentice professional with Middlesbrough in 1966, working

his way through the youth and reserve sides until a serious injury halted his progress for three months; he suffered a fractured skull in an intermediate game against Leeds United.

At seventeen, he signed as a professional and then, on his eighteenth birthday, he made his first-team debut in a 1-1 draw in a Second Division game against Millwall. Alan made three more appearances in the 1968/69 season, followed by 11 in 1969/70. In 1971, Alan starred in a superb FA Cup win over Manchester United, marking George Best out of the game at Old Trafford in a 0-0 draw, before doing the same in the Ayresome Park replay that saw Middlesbrough win 2-1. Unfortunately, the Middlesbrough crowd seemed to take a dislike to young Alan, and, in the end, the crowd abuse forced him to ask for a transfer. Arthur Rowley moved in, and Alan signed for Southend United on 10 October 1972 for a fee of £15,000. Alan started in midfield for the Blues, before switching between right-back and centre-back roles, finally settling in the heart of defence.

His first disappointment was relegation in 1975/76, which also led to the appointment of Dave Smith as Southend manager. He made Alan captain, and he led the Blues to the runner-up spot in 1977/78. The stay in the Third Division lasted only two seasons, but relega-

tion was followed by a club record-shattering season in 1980/81, when The Blues won their only major honour so far, the Fourth Division championship. As well as his Fourth Division championship medal, Alan was voted Southend United Player of the Year in 1975 and was also the inaugural winner of the club's Goal of the Season competition in 1981 – the reward for a cracking right-foot volley against Halifax in a 5-1 win. Alan was also known as a penalty king, notching 24 goals from the spot out of 28 attempts, with only one being saved, by Doncaster Rovers' Dennis Peacock in the 1977/78 season.

Alan left Southend in May 1984, joining Essex Senior League outfit Maldon Town, having recorded the most first-team appearances in a Southend United shirt ever – a record that is unlikely to be beaten. After retiring from football, Alan became secretary at Banstead Downs Golf Club, allowing him to enjoy his other passion, golf.

Billy Moore

Goalkeeper

Born: Sunderland, Tyne & Wear, 10/3/1903

Died: Sunderland, 1962

Joined: June 1925, from Leeds

First team debut: v. Watford, 25/9/25

Appearances: 304

Goals: 0

Other clubs: Seaham Colliery, 1921-23; Leeds, 1923-25; Hartlepool, 1936-37

Billy Moore was born in Sunderland at the turn of the century and first became interested in goalkeeping whilst at school. As a teenager, he was able to gain valuable practice in the art of shot stopping by working at the East End Old Market in his hometown on a 'beat the keeper' attraction. He was paid five shillings a week as punters paid a penny to take a pot shot at the young custodian.

Billy later took an apprenticeship in a local shipyard to train as a naval carpenter. He played in goal for the Limited Yard Apprentices and caught the eye of Wearside League club, Seaham Colliery. After a Seaham match against Herrington Swifts in March 1924, watched by several scouts, Blackburn Rovers' manager, R.B. Middleton, offered the youngster a trial, but Moore turned them down in order to qualify in his chosen trade. However, a few days later Arthur Fairclough, the manager of Leeds United, who was guiding his side to the Second Division title that season, offered Moore the chance of a match in Leeds' Central League side. Moore accepted the offer, but on arriving at Elland Road he found that Leeds already had three experi-enced custodians in Billy Down, Bill Johnson and David Russell.

Despite the fierce competition, Moore managed to play in 6 First Division matches in the 1924/25 campaign, keeping two clean sheets. He was popular with the crowd and his team mates, but, realising his chances were limited at Elland Road, Moore readily agreed to a move south in June 1925, Ted Birnie signing him for Southend United. He soon displaced the regular 'keeper, Billy Hayes, and made his debut at Watford towards the end of September. He was to become first choice at The Kursaal for many years, although an injury sustained against Coventry in February 1928 cost him the majority of the 1927/28 season. He came back strongly from that setback to be ever present in the following campaign, a feat he would repeat in the 1930/31 season. For the 1931/32 campaign, Ted Birnie signed another experienced goalkeeper, Dave Whitelaw, who arrived from Bristol City during the summer. Both Moore and Whitelaw vied for the 'keeper's jersey for the next four seasons. Although Whitelaw's presence would deprive him of many potential appearances, Billy Moore became only the second Blues player, after Dickie Donoven, to surpass 300 appearances for the Blues when he kept goal in a 6-1 victory against Reading in May 1935.

Billy Moore was a hugely popular and brave 'keeper who always wore his red jersey and flat cap when on the field and delighted the Kursaal crowd with his comic antics and lively banter. Although quite short for a goalkeeper at a shade under 5'10", he was tremendously agile and would often dive acrobatically to make a routine save look spectacular for the benefit of the Southend supporters. He was also considered to be quite a heartthrob amongst the female populace of the town and gained further celebrity status by playing the piano in dance bands in local halls and clubs. He would also entertain his club mates by tinkling the ivories at squad functions.

One particular incident in 1932 highlighted what a proud man Billy Moore was. After a skirmish in his penalty area, Moore struck an opponent and was ordered from the field by the referee. So ashamed of his behaviour, Moore removed his jersey and tied it around his face to avoid sharing his disgrace with the crowd. His loyalty was rewarded with a benefit match against Everton in April 1931, when the legendary Dixie Dean ran the line as he was not fit enough to play. In 1936, new manager David Jack, concerned about Moore's increasing susceptibility to injury, decided to buy a new goalkeeper. It was a testament to Moore's reputation that Jack replaced him with a future Ireland international, George Mackenzie, from Plymouth. Moore announced his intention to retire at the end of that season, but Hartlepool's late offer change his mind and he enjoyed a further campaign of League action.

After a truly colourful career Moore returned to his roots by working in a North East shipyard for many years. Sadly, Billy Moore was only fifty-nine when he passed away in 1962.

Gary Moore
Striker

Born: South Hetton, Co. Durham, 4/11/1945

Joined: October 1968, from Grimbsy

First team debut: v. York, 19/10/68

Appearances: 172(9)

Goals: 55

Other clubs: Sunderland, 1962-66; Grimsby, 1966-68; Chester, 1974-75; Swansea, 1976-77

Gary Moore had his critics. However, he is still one of only seventeen players to score more than fifty goals for The Shrimpers since League status was attained in 1920. Moore gained representative honours first with Sunderland boys and then for Durham County boys. He signed as an amateur for Sunderland at the age of fifteen and, a year later, played for England youth. He made steady progress through the ranks at Roker Park and signed professional forms in 1962, when he had turned seventeen. However, Moore managed only 13 appearances in four seasons for Sunderland and was sold to Grimsby in July 1966. The board had forced manager Jimmy McGuigan to sell top scorer Rod Green and legendary goal-getter Matt Tees and Moore faced an uphill struggle to replace two hugely popular figures. This, coupled with bad luck with injuries, meant his time with the Mariners was not successful.

Southend's manager, Ernie Shepherd, felt he needed a tall target man to complement Billy Best and brought Gary Moore to Roots Hall. Within a month of his arrival, Moore was making headlines. He scored a hat-trick against Kings Lynn in the first round of the FA Cup, and then struck four goals in an astonishing 10-1 win over Brentwood in the second round. In a nutshell, that game proved Moore's worth – despite his gangly appearance he was remarkably strong

in the air and was to prove a perfect foil for Best. Moore scored another hat-trick in a League match against Swansea Town in April 1969 and finished the campaign with 21 goals, as the Blues hit an incredible 106 goals in all competitions.

After a prolific start to his Roots Hall career, much was expected of Moore, but the next four seasons each saw him fail to make double figures. The 1970/71 campaign was particularly forgettable as he missed the first three months after breaking his knee-cap. However, Moore's hold-up play and flick-ons did create many chances for others. The start of the 1973/74 season saw The Blues with a poor scoring record in the opening ten fixtures and, in an attempt to improve firepower, Arthur Rowley signed Stuart Brace and Willy Coulson. With the competition for places, Moore lost his position and was loaned to Colchester for the rest of the season.

Strangely, despite Moore scoring seven times and assisting the U's to a promotion place from the Fourth Division, Jim Smith did not pursue his interest in the striker. In the summer of 1974, Moore joined Chester on a free transfer, and after two seasons left for Swansea, but he never rediscovered his goalscoring touch. It is a great shame that many Blues fans will remember Gary Moore for his lack of ball control and poor distribution rather than for his contribution to an extraordinary season in the history of Southend.

Colin Morris
Midfielder

Born: Blyth, Northumberland, 22/8/1953

Joined: January 1977, from Burnley

First team debut: v. Stockport, 28/1/77

Appearances: 156

Goals: 30

Other clubs: Burnley, 1971-75; Blackpool, 1979-81; Sheffield Utd, 1982-87; Scarborough, 1988-89

Colin Morris was a fine right-sided midfielder, who supplied pinpoint crosses with either foot. He also contributed a healthy total of goals himself, having an especially fruitful season during the 1977/78 campaign, when he scored 13 times as The Blues won promotion to the Third Division. A particularly notable performance came in January 1978, when Bournemouth were torn apart at Roots Hall. Morris scored twice and was instrumental in the moves that resulted in goals for Gerry Fell, Peter Abbott and Micky Laverick as the Cherries were beaten 5-1. It came as no real surprise that Morris was voted Player of the Year at the end of that season.

Morris had begun his career as an apprentice with Burnley in September 1971 and he duly turned professional in the summer of 1973, but had to wait until January 1975 to make his first-team debut. He made a single further appearance that season, however, the following season, Morris played 8 games, but the competition for places meant his opportunities were extremely limited. When Joe Brown took over as manager for the 1976/77 campaign, Morris was banished to the reserves and he realised he needed a move.

In January 1977 Morris arrived at Roots Hall. After he had played more than 150 games in a Blues shirt, manager Dave Smith, having obtained the services of Terry Gray reluctantly felt he could cash in on his valuable midfielder.

In a shrewd move, Smith purchased the prolific striker, Derek Spence, from Blackpool and when the Seasiders boss, Bob Stokoe, offered to return the fee in exchange for the signature of Morris, all parties were more than happy. Morris had two outstanding seasons at Bloomfield Road, but February 1982 saw a move to Sheffield United, where Ian Porterfield saw him as the missing piece of his jigsaw, and Morris helped the team to the Fourth Division title. He became a legend at Bramall Lane and scored 20 goals as the Blades won promotion again in 1983/84.

Throughout his time at Sheffield United, Morris was the regular penalty taker. He set the club record for most successful spot kicks (48) and also the most misses (12). At the start of 1988 though, Morris found himself unable to hold a regular place in the side under their new manager, Dave Bassett. Scarborough were in only their second season in the League when Morris joined them, initially as a player-coach, but when Neil Warnock departed, Morris was offered a player-manager role. Morris accepted the post at Seamer Road and guided the club to the play-offs at the end of the 1988/89 season.

Colin Morris was a midfielder of genuine class and was no doubt extremely proud of his young son, Lee, who became Britain's most expensive teenager when Derby County signed him for £3 million from Sheffield United in 1999.

Garry Nelson
Striker

Born: Braintree, Essex, 16/1/1961

Joined: July 1979, from juniors

First team debut: v. Colchester, 12/10/79

Appearances: 118(26)

Goals: 18

Other clubs: Swindon, 1983-85; Plymouth Argyle, 1985-87; Brighton & Hove Albion, 1987-90; Charlton Athletic, 1991-96; Torquay, 1996-97

Garry was born in Braintree in 1961 and joined Southend United as an amateur before signing professional forms in the summer of 1979. Although he went on to make over 100 first-team appearances for the Blues, Garry never really got the backing he deserved from the fans.

During the 1979/80 campaign and the championship season of 1980/81, Nelson often found himself on the substitutes' bench or, if he had actually started a game, he was the one that would make way for a replacement. The 1981/2 season saw Nelson gain a more regular place in the Blues line-up. However, it was his final season at Roots Hall, 1982/83, that would prove to be his best in a Blues shirt, when he played in all but one match. He also contributed his best goals tally for Southend (9), finishing as joint second-top goalscorer.

Nelson decided to leave Southend in the close season and moved in August 1983, to join Swindon Town, where he played two seasons under player-manager Lou Macari. In July 1985, Garry linked up with his old boss from Southend, Dave Smith at Plymouth, and his career began to blossom. Given free reign to explore the left-hand side of the pitch, his natural ability came to the fore and he starred in the Plymouth Argyle promotion-winning team of 1985/86, helping the Pilgrims reach the Second Division and bag-

ging 14 goals in the process. An injury-hit campaign followed, before he again moved on, this time to another seaside resort, Brighton.

Garry rattled in 27 goals in 1987/88, which helped Brighton to runners-up spot and promotion to the Second Division. In fact, the only player to score more goals than Garry in the whole division during that campaign was Southend's David Crown. After a couple more seasons at Brighton, and a very brief loan spell at Notts County in November 1990, Garry made the move to Charlton Athletic in August 1991. Garry made over 150 appearances for the Addicks, all in the top flight, and finished as their top scorer in the 1993/1994 campaign.

The lure of the West Country was too much, however, and, in August 1996, he responded to an invitation from Kevin Hodges to become player-coach at Torquay United. When Garry's playing career finally ended, he took the unusual step of writing two books, *Left Foot Forward* and *Left Foot in the Grave*, about his playing experiences in the lower reaches of the Football League; both went on to become bestsellers.

As befits a man who made nearly 650 League appearances in his career, Garry found a job with the Professional Football Association, allowing him to pass on the knowledge he learnt through his seventeen-year career. He remains a fine player for veteran sides.

Ricky Otto
Striker

Born: Hackney, East London, 9/11/67

Joined: July 1993, from Leyton Orient

First team debut: v. Nottingham Forest, 15/8/93

Appearances: 75(1)

Goals: 19

Other clubs: Dartford, 1988-89; Haringey Borough, 1989-90; Leyton Orient, 1990-92; Birmingham, 1994-95; Halesowen Town, 2000-2001

Ricky Otto was a bit of a tearaway as a youngster and, although a prodigiously skilful footballer, his personal life meant that League scouts overlooked his ability, deeming him too much of a risk. However, Otto decided to make a go of a career in football and joined part-timers Haringey Borough in 1989. There he came to the attention of Leyton Orient's manager, Frank Clark, who signed him for the O's in November 1990, but Otto had to wait until the final game of that season to make his League debut.

Over the next two seasons, Otto became a popular figure, playing nearly 70 first-team games. He was keen to play at a higher level and joined Southend in July 1993. Otto made his Blues debut in the opening game of the 1993/94 season. The Blues needed a new hero following the decline in popularity of Brett Angell, who had upset supporters with comments about wanting to leave the club. Otto possessed the skill and trickery to become an idol at Roots Hall and he succeeded with some exciting wing play as well as important goals. He was leading scorer with 15 League and cup goals in his first campaign.

His outrageous ball control often meant that Otto would come in for some harsh treatment from embarrassed defenders. In an Anglo-Italian Cup match in Italy against Cosenza, Otto had continually outwitted his marker. Barry Fry, fearing for his winger's safety, was forced into substituting Otto to protect him from lasting injury. However, as the Blues team walked down the tunnel of the San Vito stadium after a 2-1 triumph, his adversary charged towards Otto with a hammer. Fortunately for Otto, Southend's player-coach, Dave Howell, a huge bear of a man, intercepted the enraged Italian and forced him to drop his weapon. Ricky Otto continued to enthral Shrimpers fans before he followed Barry Fry to Birmingham in December 1994 for a sizeable fee of £800,000.

He had a memorable debut for City, scoring at both ends in a 1-1 draw with Cambridge. At St Andrews, Fry was often forced to employ Otto as an orthodox centre forward and his unfamiliarity with the role left him frustrated. To make matters worse, the City fans did not take him to their hearts. Following Fry's dismissal, Otto became surplus to requirements and found himself loaned to Charlton and then Peterborough, where he was reunited with Barry Fry, although a permanent move was never agreed.

The start of the 1997/98 season saw Otto loaned again, this time to Notts County. However, he soon sustained a cruciate ligament injury and the damage was so severe that it eventually led to the end of Otto's colourful and dramatic career, although he did resurface on the football front with a brief stint at Halesowen Town during the 2000/01 season.

Anton Otulakowski

Midfielder

Born: Dewsbury, West Yorkshire, 29/1/1956

Joined: March 1979, from West Ham

First team debut: v, Watford, 2/4/79

Appearances: 187(2)

Goals: 8

Other clubs: Ossett Trinity, 1974-75; Barnsley, 1975-76; West Ham, 1976-77; Millwall, 1983-85; Crystal Palace, 1986-87

Anton Otulakowski was eighteen when he was snapped up by Barnsley. He made his League debut in the last game of the 1974/75 Fourth Division campaign. The following season, Otulakowski had to bide his time before being called into the first team in November and then played all of the remaining 32 games of the season, scoring twice. The start of the 1976/77 season saw him in sparkling form, his outstanding control and athletic body swerve having been developed while he was a schoolboy competing in gymnastic competitions at a national level. By October 1976, Barnsley were resigned to losing their starlet and he moved to West Ham United.

Despite stiff competition in the Hammers midfield, the Yorkshireman made a dozen appearances before an injury in early April ended his season. The 1977/78 campaign saw Otulakowski again crowded out of the team, being restricted to only 5 substitute appearances. Otulakowski was hoping to figure more following the side's demotion, but soon realized he needed to look elsewhere for regular first-team football.

In March 1979, he signed for Southend. Otulakowski was outstanding in his first full campaign for the Blues, the 1979/80 season, despite the club suffering relegation to the Fourth Division. An injury in pre-season meant he missed the start of the epic 1980/81 season.

However, once installed on the left side of midfield, Otulakowski was again outstanding, his deft skill and accurate crosses and corners providing many goalscoring chances as Southend swept aside all before them to win the Fourth Division championship and return to the Third Division at the first attempt. At around this time, Otulakowski used his suppleness to perfect a party-piece throw-in. Although the move was outlawed in the League, friendly matches on pitches with sufficient room outside the touchline saw the midfielder clutch the ball behind his head, as if preparing for a normal throw-in, then perform a handstand and land on both feet, using the extra leverage to hurl the ball back into play with prodigious distance and velocity.

Otulakowski played consistently well for Southend over the next two seasons, but in March 1983 he was sold to Millwall. The move angered manager Dave Smith so much that he fell out with the club's owners and the incident precipitated his shock departure a few months later. Otulakowski spend three successful seasons at The Den and then transferred to Crystal Palace for the 1986/87 season. Sadly, in a match in November 1986, Otulakowski sustained a serious knee injury that was to end his career. He remained involved in the game by running highly successful coaching schools in the Southend area for many years.

Derrick Parker
Striker

Born: Wallsend, Tyne & Wear, 7/2/1957

Joined: February 1977, from Burnley

First team debut: v. Workington, 12/2/77

Appearances: 149

Goals: 51

Other clubs: Burnley, 1974-75 & 1985-86; Barnsley, 1979-82; Oldham Athletic, 1983-84; Oulon Pallasuera (Finland), 1986-87; Rochdale, 1987-88

Derrick was playing for Wallsend boys, at the age of fifteen, having already represented Northumberland boys, when he was approached by three clubs for his signature. Both Liverpool and Coventry City missed out, as Derrick decided to join his friend, Ray Hankin, at Burnley, and he made his first-team debut at the age of seventeen in March 1975.

Four more starts and one goal saw Derrick finish the season as a first-team player. Unfortunately for Derrick, the 1975/76 season was not so good, as not only were Burnley relegated from the top flight, but he was relegated to the reserves. Derrick played only one match and, although he scored, Burnley lost 1-3 to Coventry City and were relegated. The 1976/77 campaign saw Derrick playing in midfield for Burnley reserves, so he was relieved when Southend manager Dave Smith offered him a chance to come to Roots Hall.

Initially joining on loan for a month, Derrick scored in his opening two League appearances for The Blues, and was snapped up by Smith at the end of the loan period. Derrick played every game until the end of the season, forming an excellent understanding with his colleagues. The 1977/78 season saw the Blues finish as runners-up in the Fourth Division, and Derrick was top scorer, notching 23 League and cup goals without missing a game. His highlight came in September 1977, when he scored all the goals in a 4-0 home victory over Torquay United.

The following year was harder for The Blues, but Derrick still managed to finish as top scorer, his 12 League and cup goals being the only double-figure return at the club that season. Derrick left The Blues halfway through the 1979/80 campaign, joining Barnsley, but he had still managed enough goals to be top scorer for the third consecutive season – a feat only achieved by four others. Derrick scored on his debut for Barnsley and the following season scored 10 goals, helping The Tykes to runners-up spot in the Third Division. Derrick found the 1981/82 campaign in the Second Division much harder, and played only 18 games, scoring 6 goals, but the following season was better, and he scored 11 goals – including one in the 3-0 victory at Stamford Bridge against Chelsea.

During the close season, Derrick transferred to Oldham Athletic and spent two seasons at Boundary Park before returning to his first club, Burnley, via a loan spell at Doncaster Rovers, in October 1985. After leaving Turf Moor for the second time, Derrick had a spell in Finland before returning, for a brief period, in October 1987 with Rochdale. Exactly 100 League goals in a career spanning 354 appearances for six different clubs was an exceptional return for a truly underrated striker.

Glenn Pennyfather

Midfielder

Born: Billericay, Essex, 11/2/1963

Joined: February 1981, from apprentice

First team debut: v. Hereford, 22/11/80

Appearances: 265(8)

Goals: 43

Other clubs: Crystal Palace, 1987-89; Ipswich, 1989-93; Bristol City, 1993-94; Canvey Island, 1994-97

The growth of Glenn Pennyfather into a classy midfielder was a ray of light in the overwhelming gloom that surrounded the club in the early 1980s, following the departure of Dave Smith as manager in June 1983. The youngster had signed apprentice forms with the Blues in 1979 and his progress was rapid. By November 1980, with Pennyfather still only seventeen, Smith felt he was ready for first-team action and selected him for the FA Cup first round tie against Hereford United. Later that month he played in the League match against Doncaster, but Pennyfather really came to the fore in the 1981/82 season, gaining a regular first-team place. He continued to improve in his central midfield role, although the club again lost their Third Division place, at the end of the 1983/84 season.

The 1984/85 season was arguably the worst in the club's history, the Blues avoiding the ignominy of applying for re-election by virtue of having a slightly less appalling goal difference than Halifax Town. Pennyfather, however, had contributed a personal best seasonal tally of 7 – a figure he repeated in the following campaign when the Blues finished in a more respectable ninth place. The 1986/87 season, under new manager Dave Webb, saw The Blues, and Pennyfather, excel themselves. Pennyfather scored 14 goals as Southend secured promotion.

Crystal Palace offered £150,000 for his services in November 1987 and the club did not stand in his way. The fee was the highest paid for a Blues player since the same club had prised Peter Taylor away back in 1973. His two seasons at Selhurst Park were blighted by injury and he moved to Ipswich Town in October 1989.

Disaster struck in October 1990 when Pennyfather sustained a serious knee injury which would keep him sidelined until the end of the following campaign. The following two seasons saw very brief spells in the team, coupled with lengthy spells in the treatment room. In March 1993, Pennyfather was sold for £80,000 to Bristol City and had an injury-free run for the remainder of the campaign, although City's manager, Russell Osman, played him in an unfamiliar right-back position. The 1993/94 season saw injuries rear their head once more, restricting Pennyfather to 12 Football League appearances. City cancelled his registration before the end of the campaign, allowing him to return to Essex and take up a full-time teaching job.

Pennyfather continued to play football, being a driving force behind Canvey Island's meteoric rise from the Essex Senior League to the upper reaches of the Ryman League. He retired from playing in 1997, but stayed on at Canvey as first-team coach, guiding the Islanders to the FA Trophy final in 2001.

Steve Phillips
Striker

Born: Edmonton, North London, 4/8/1954

Joined: March 1982, from Northampton

First team debut: v. Chesterfield, 5/3/82

Appearances: 180(2)

Goals: 72

Other clubs: Birmingham, 1971-75; Northampton, 1975-77 & 1980-82; Brentford, 1977-80; Torquay, 1985-86; Peterborough, 1986-88

When Steve Phillips arrived at Roots Hall in March 1982 he faced the onerous task of filling the void left by popular frontman Derek Spence. Phillips was the antithesis of the tall, blond Spence – being short and stocky, he was known as 'Inchy'. Although born in London, Phillips was offered an apprenticeship at Birmingham City and soon gained England youth caps. He made his debut just after his seventeenth birthday in August 1971, but only appeared another six times before being dropped back into the reserves. Over the next four campaigns he made a handful of appearances in each season, but was unable to displace household names such as Trevor Francis and Kenny Burns.

In the 1974/75 season he was loaned to Torquay briefly, before he joined Northampton Town, initially on loan, before signing a permanent contract. He was fairly successful at the County Ground, despite often being employed in a midfield role. Moving to Brentford in February 1977, he was again used in midfield for a while. However, the Bees' boss decided to use Phillips as a forward for the 1977/78 season. The switch was a success, with Brentford gaining promotion. Phillips was ever present that season and finished top scorer with 32 goals. He top scored again for the next two campaigns and became a legend, scoring nearly 80 League and cup goals before rejoining Northampton in June 1980.

Phillips was ever-present during his first campaign back at the County Ground, scoring 22 goals. He was leading scorer in 1981/82, despite joining Southend in March 1982. He made his debut in a 2-0 defeat against Chesterfield, but in the remaining 17 matches of the season, Phillips scored 10 goals. He was the Blues' leading scorer for the next three seasons. Arguably Phillips' most important goal in a Blues shirt came in the final game of the 1984/85 season. The Blues entered the game knowing that defeat would mean having to rely on the re-election ballot. In a tense match against bottom-of-the-table Torquay, the Blues were terrible. They were, however, handed a lifeline when the referee awarded a dubious penalty. Phillips' spot kick hit the inside of the right-hand goal post and rolled along the goal line, finally trickling into the net. The Blues survived, finishing ahead of Halifax by virtue of a slightly better goal difference.

Phillips started the 1985/86 campaign as a first-choice striker, but when Roy McDonough and Richard Cadette suddenly clicked, Phillips was offloaded to Torquay. He then had a spell at Peterborough, during which he was loaned to Exeter and Chesterfield. He was released in the close season and wound down his career with Eastern Counties League Stamford. He worked as a double-glazing salesman for several years, but currently lives in Spain, where he owns a bar.

Ronnie Pountney
Midfielder

Born: Bilston, West Midlands, 19/3/1955

Joined: January 1975, from Bilston

First team debut: v. Swindon, 11/4/75

Appearances: 376(25)

Goals: 35

Other clubs: Walsall, 1972-73; Port Vale, 1973-74; Bilston, 1974-75; Chelmsford, 1985-86 & 1987-88; Heybridge Swifts, 1986-87; Gravesend & Northfleet, 1988-89, Dartford, 1989-90

It would be interesting if a dictionary of football clichés was ever published. The often used quote of 'small in stature, big in heart' would surely figure in such a tome – and there could be no better analogy applied to legendary Blues midfielder Ronnie Pountney. A frail figure, standing 5' 6" tall, and with a weight of less than 10 stone, he did not have the typical build of a professional footballer. Pountney was born into a large family of West Bromwich Albion supporters and was christened Ronald Alan after the West Brom and England forward, Ronnie Allen. A seventeen-year-old Pountney turned up at Fellows Park for a trial with Walsall. He was taken on and played in the League match against Scunthorpe in April 1973. However, a change of manager saw the young midfielder released by the new man in charge – none other than Ronnie Allen.

By the following campaign, Pountney had impressed enough in pre-season to earn a contract at Port Vale. However, he failed to break into the first team and was again released, with Vale manager Gordon Lee not convinced he would make the grade with such a slight frame. The dejected youngster returned home and

signed for West Midland League outfit Bilston. He had an outstanding season for the non-Leaguers and attracted the attention of Southend manager Arthur Rowley, who signed him in January 1975 for a fee of £3,000. Bilston used the money from the sale to build a clubhouse at their Queen Street ground. At first, Pountney struggled to adapt to the rigours of full-time training, but Rowley considered him ready and played him in the last four games of the 1974/75 campaign. The next three seasons saw Pountney figure in about half the games Southend played, as he tried to gain a regular place in the side. He had been shocked by the departure of Rowley at the end of the 1975/76 season, but was to blossom under the shrewd management of Dave Smith.

Pountney really made the breakthrough in the 1978/79 season, playing all but four of the League matches and all the cup matches, including the two memorable FA Cup ties against Liverpool. The match at Roots Hall against the European champions saw Pountney gain rave reviews for his man-to-man marking of Ray Kennedy. Pountney was voted Player of the Year at the end of that season, a title he retained the following campaign – despite the Blues being relegated to the Fourth Division. The 1980/81 season saw Southend storm to the Fourth Division title, shattering many club

records, and he was again outstanding, missing only two matches in the club's greatest campaign. In 1982/83, Pountney won a club record third Player of the Year award and was ever-present during 56 first-team matches. The little midfielder gave particularly memorable performances in the FA Cup. In the second round, against renowned giant-killers Yeovil Town, Blues avoided the potential embarrassment of a third FA Cup defeat to the Somerset side with Pountney in devastating form, scoring twice as Southend outplayed the non-Leaguers for a 3-0 victory. In the third round, Pountney scored a last-minute equaliser in a replay against Sheffield Wednesday – sadly, Blues lost the coin toss for venue advantage and went down 1-2 at Hillsborough in the second replay.

By the end of the 1984/85 campaign, Pountney had amassed 401 appearances in a Blues shirt, the fourth highest total in the club's long history. The player's unswerving loyalty to the club was rewarded with a testimonial season that year, but the highlight, a

testimonial match against West Ham, was postponed due to the Hammers' fixture pile-up that year and Southend manager Bobby Moore gave Pountney a free transfer before the game could be rearranged. The midfielder was still only thirty when he signed for Chelmsford City. After leaving Roots Hall, he established his own painting and decorating firm and carried on playing for several non-League clubs.

Ronnie remains a fine veteran player for Fords Basildon and Courtlands and still lives in Eastwood. After a concerted campaign by the resurgent Southend United Supporters' Club, the midfielder had his testimonial match, some fourteen years late, staged in August 2000 against Charlton Athletic. A veterans match prior to the main game saw the return to Roots Hall of the majority of the 1980/81 championship-winning side. This was an emotional night for all concerned and, along with the memorabilia auction, raised £25,000 for one of Southend United's all-time most popular and respected figures.

Chris Powell

Defender

Born: Lambeth, London, 8/9/1969

Joined: July 1990, from Crystal Palace

First team debut: v. Crewe, 1/9/90

Appearances: 288(2)

Goals: 3

Other clubs: Crystal Palace, 1987-90; Derby County, 1995-97; Charlton Athletic, 1998-2001

In many books such as this, the term 'popular' is often used to describe much-loved players, but surely there is no more suitable adjective to ascribe to Chris Powell. The Lambeth-born left-back came through the ranks at Crystal Palace and was offered professional terms by Steve Coppell in December 1987. The promising youngster had to wait until regular left-back, David Burke, was injured to get his chance. He made his debut in November 1988 against Barnsley and kept his place for the next match at Bournemouth. He then dropped down to the bench, when his place in the starting line-up was taken, ironically, by another Southend legend, Glenn Pennyfather. Burke recovered from injury to regain his place and, later, Coppell signed Mark Dennis and also converted Richard Shaw from centre-back to left-back.

With Powell's first-team opportunities at Selhurst Park becoming increasingly restricted, he accepted Len Walker's offer of a loan move to Aldershot in January 1990. He played eleven games at either left-back or the left-side of midfield, including a 5-0 defeat at Roots Hall, but the offer of a permanent move to the Recreation Ground was not forthcoming. Coppell, with a squad overloaded with defenders, handed the young left-back a free transfer at the end of the 1989/90 season.

Southend manager Dave Webb was searching for a new left-back to replace Justin Edinburgh, who had been sold to Tottenham for £150,000 that summer, and Powell fitted the bill perfectly. He became an instant hit with the Blues faithful, endearing himself with a nifty dance-move 'wiggle', which was to become a trademark. He became a regular in the side that gained promotion to the Second Division for the first time in the club's history. He did, however, lose his place in the team to Christian Hyslop for the final three matches of the run-in, including the historic victory at Bury – where Powell was only a substitute. Powell developed into a superbly consistent performer, missing only 8 of Southend's next 211 League matches, and eventually clocking up a total of 290 appearances.

He had many admirable qualities, always playing with a ready smile and taking time to sign autographs and pose for photographs with young supporters. His level of performance and skill was recognised by several clubs and Jim Smith signed him for Derby County in January 1996 for £800,000. It was a blow to Southend, but many supporters were pleased that Powell

had finally earned a shot at the big time. Derby gained promotion to the Premiership and he was voted the Rams' Player of the Year in his first full season in the top flight. In July 1998, Powell moved back to South London as Alan Curbishley invested £850,000 of Charlton's transfer budget on a player who now had over 400 appearances behind him. He became a vital member of the Athletic side that stormed to the Division One title in 1999/2000, and his consistency was recognised by his fellow professionals, as he was included in the PFA Division One side for that campaign.

He comfortably readjusted to life in the Premiership and his major skills of raiding left-flank charges and the ability to manoeuvre attacking players into less threatening positions became well noted. However, many journalists still raised an eyebrow when he was named in Sven Goran Eriksson's first England squad in February 2001 for the friendly game against Spain. The surprise was doubled when he actually made the starting eleven. His outstanding performance in neutralising the considerable threat of a world-class attacking midfielder, Valencia's Gaizka Mendieta, filled many column inches in the national press. Of course, it came as no surprise at all to Southend fans, who were filled with pride as 'our boy came good'.

Trevor Roberts
Goalkeeper

Born: Caernarfon, Gwyned, 25/2/1942

Died: 1972

Joined: January 1966, from Liverpool

First team debut: v. Mansfield, 8/1/66

Appearances: 188

Goals: 0

Other clubs: Liverpool, 1963-66; Cambridge Utd, 1970-71

Born in North Wales, in February 1942, Trevor Roberts gained 3 Welsh under-18 youth caps before putting the idea of becoming a professional footballer to the back of his mind. Instead, he went to Liverpool University to study Geography and kept goal for the university team. Whilst playing for them he was spotted by Bill Shankly, who signed him as an amateur, allowing Roberts to complete his studies and gain 9 Welsh amateur international caps.

Once he had graduated, Trevor signed professional forms at Anfield in June 1963, travelling as the reserve 'keeper for Liverpool's European Cup Winners Cup match at Juventus in the 1965/66 season. However, the remarkably consistent form of Scottish international Tommy Lawrence meant that Roberts never got a chance to make a first-team appearance and he eventually joined Southend United in January 1966, halfway through a relegation season. Immediately taking over from the erratic Ian McKechnie, Roberts made his debut against Mansfield in January 1966, keeping a clean sheet in a 1-0 victory.

Remarkably, although he had no experience at League level, his form was exceptional, and he went on to make 109 consecutive appearances in the first team, before losing his place for a single game to Ray White in the 1967/68 season. The 1966/67 season was defensively the best in the club's history to that point, with only 49 goals

conceded in 46 games, and it came as no surprise when Roberts was voted Player of the Year. This was a fitting reward for an outstanding season, which saw Roberts keep a remarkable fourteen clean sheets. His commanding performances were complemented by a rock-steady defence. The 1967/68 campaign saw Blues again miss out on promotion, but Roberts kept another ten clean sheets, including three straight shut-outs against Luton, Swansea and Hartlepool during September. Having started the 1968/69 season as second choice to Lawrie Leslie, Trevor won his place back when Leslie suffered a fractured arm in October 1968. Roberts went on to make 37 appearances that season, including playing the role of virtual spectator in two FA Cup matches – the 9-0 win over Kings Lynn and the 10-1 demolition of Brentwood.

Roberts shared the number one jersey with Brian Lloyd during the 1969/70 season, and left in August 1970 to join Cambridge United, who had just been elected to the Football League. He left Roots Hall with an total of 48 clean sheets and the reputation of being one of Southend's greatest ever custodians. Roberts made his Cambridge debut in their first League fixture, a 1-1 draw against Lincoln City, but after only 36 League appearances, and at the tragically young age of thirty, he died of a brain tumour in 1972.

Dave Robinson
Defender

Born: Longton, Dumfries & Galloway, c.1900

Died: 1986

Joined: May 1928, from Leeds

First team debut: v. Bournemouth, 25/8/28

Appearances: 348

Goals: 1

Other clubs: Lockerbie, 1917-19; Eskdale, 1919-21; Workington, 1921-22; Carlisle, 1922-23; Solway Star, 1923-26; Leeds, 1926-28

Dave Robinson was born in Longton, Dumfries and Galloway, around the beginning of the twentieth century (although his exact date of birth has never been established). He spent the early part of his football career with Scottish junior sides Lockerbie and Eskdale. In June 1921, he joined non-League Workington, who were plying their trade in the North-Eastern League – a competition of considerable standing at the time.

Robinson spent only a season at Lonsdale Park before joining fellow North-Eastern Leaguers Carlisle United. Again, Robinson failed to establish himself as a regular and returned to his native Dumfrieshire with Solway Star in July 1923. The club, now known as Annan Athletic, were embarking on their first season as a Scottish League club in the ill-fated first incarnation of the Scottish Third Division. Robinson played for Solway for all three of their campaigns, before the division was abandoned in 1926. The full-back had played well enough to attract the attention of Arthur Fairclough, who signed Robinson for his Leeds United side.

He made his official debut for Leeds on 9 October 1926 in a 4-1 win over Blackburn at Elland Road. He made a further three League appearances that season, but the following campaign saw Robinson play only one

match. He was, not surprisingly, released from the Yorkshire club in the summer of 1928. Robinson, by now, must have been wondering whether he would ever really make the grade as a professional player. In truth he was a most unlikely looking player, standing only 5' 5" tall and weighing nearly 12 stone. It was, therefore, with no little trepidation that the Scotsman headed south to sign up with Southend United for the 1928/29 season.

Robinson blossomed under the watchful eye of manager Ted Birnie and became equally adept at either full-back berth. He also perfected the difficult art of the sliding tackle, but his wholehearted style meant the little man suffered his fair share of injuries, including a particularly serious leg injury sustained in 1933. His now-burgeoning career had another setback in September 1934, when he and two of his Southend team-mates, Joe Wilson and Bert Jones, were arrested for rabbit poaching. At the court hearing, all three were found guilty and, for his part, Robinson was fined ten shillings and had his firearms impounded.

Dave Robinson surpassed Dickie Donoven's club record for appearances during the 1938/39

season and went on to set a new record of 348 by the end of that campaign. It was this season that the full-back finally broke his goal drought for the Blues, scoring in a 5-0 demolition of Newport County in what was his 347th game for the club. His appearance record stood unbroken until the late 1950s, when overhauled by fellow Scot Sandy Anderson.

Robinson's long career was ended in 1940, when he broke his leg in a wartime match against Norwich City. It was the second such injury of his playing career – while he was with Leeds, the tough Scotsman had played on a broken leg for some forty minutes in a match against Leicester. After the war, Robinson became Harry Warren's assistant trainer, a post he held for thirteen years. He then took a job on the Roots Hall groundstaff, and was still doing odd jobs around the ground when he died in August 1986. Robinson's fifty-eight-year association with Southend United was rewarded with a benefit match against Oxford United in 1961, and a testimonial match against Aston Villa in 1970.

Arthur Rowley
Manager

Born: Wolverhampton, West Midlands, 21/4/1926

Joined: March 1970 as manager

Other clubs: Wolverhampton Wanderers, 1942-44; West Brom, 1944-48; Fulham, 1948-50; Leicester, 1950-58; Shrewsbury, 1958-65

Arthur Rowley holds a unique place in football folklore as the most prolific goalscorer in League history. His record of 434 goals in 619 appearances is unlikely to be threatened, considering Ian Wright – generally regarded as one of the greatest marksmen of the modern era – ended some 200 goals adrift of Rowley's figure. As a youth he was due to play a trial match for England schoolboys when war broke out. Unbelievably, Rowley joined his brother, Jack in a wartime fixture for Manchester United when he was still only fourteen. He then joined the Army, after which Rowley had brief spells at Wolves and West Brom but, remarkably, was released without being tried in the first team.

He then moved to Fulham where his proficiency in front of goal became apparent, as he bagged 19 goals in 22 matches. However, a broken toe hampered his second season. In July 1950, Leicester signed Rowley and he went on to score at an astonishing rate for the next six years. He continued in a similar vein when he moved to Shrewsbury as player-manager in June 1958. During his career at Gay Meadow, he beat Dixie Dean's record of scoring 20 or more League goals for ten consecutive seasons. It was always a surprise that Arthur Rowley never followed his brother, Jack, into the England team. Perhaps his rumbustious style of play was overlooked in favour of more technically accomplished forwards. However, he did score for England 'B' in a 4-1 victory over their counterparts from Switzerland in 1956.

Rowley hung up his boots at the end of the 1964/65 season, but remained as manager until he took over the reins at Sheffield United in July 1968. However, his relationship with the board at Bramall Lane was strained from day one and disillusioned by his treatment from the club, Rowley turned his back on the game to concentrate on horseracing. However, in March 1970, when the Southend chairman was looking to replace his manager, Rowley answered the call.

Rowley signed on with the Blues and was initially a success at Roots Hall, managing to get the team back to the Third Division in 1971/72. However, for the next three seasons Southend were never better than mid-table and when the team struggled during the 1975/76 season, the fans turned on him. Not even a run to the fifth round of the FA Cup could save Rowley. Dave Smith was brought in during May 1976 and Rowley soon departed to become assistant manager at Telford United. He later managed Oswestry Town. In 1995, he was rewarded with another testimonial match when Shrewsbury played Wolves. He still lives in the Shropshire town. Despite his average record in charge of the Blues, his extraordinary career still sees him held in high regard by many Southend supporters.

Paul Sansome
Goalkeeper

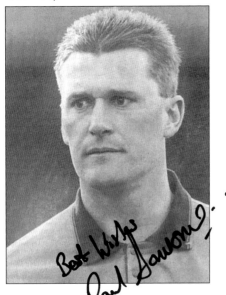

Born: New Addington, Surrey, 6/10/1961

Joined: March 1988, from Millwall

First team debut: v. Chesterfield, 25/3/88

Appearances: 357

Goals: 0

Other clubs: Crystal Palace, 1978-80; Millwall, 1980-88; Gravesend & Northfleet, 1997-98

Throughout Southend's history, the club have had a succession of goalkeeping legends, including Billy Moore, Harry Threadgold, and Mervyn Cawston. Cawston left in March 1984 and, except for an excellent couple of seasons in the capable hands of Jim Stannard, Southend never really replaced him until the arrival of Paul Sansome. Sansome started his career at Crystal Palace, but failed to break into the first team. He joined Millwall in April 1980, but it took him until the 1982/83 season to become first-choice 'keeper. He remained as such until November 1986, when Lions boss John Docherty installed the young Brian Horne between the posts for the remainder of that campaign. When Horne retained his place for the 1987/88 season, Sansome moved to Roots Hall, initially on loan, in March 1988, although his season was to finish abruptly after six matches when he was found to have played most of a game against York with a broken jaw.

Sansome's instant authority came as a great relief for Blues fans, who had suffered the comical goalkeeping of Eric Steele. In the summer of 1988, Sansome signed a permanent deal and became the undisputed number one at Roots Hall. He was ever-present throughout the successive promotions Southend achieved under Dave Webb in 1989/90 and 1990/91. He would have remained an ever-present for a third consecutive season – Southend's inaugural Second Division campaign – but for a one-game suspension, received after he had been harshly sent off against Middlesbrough.

Over the next two seasons, Sansome held off the considerable challenge of the impressive youngster, Simon Royce. During the 1994/95 season, with Southend's safety in Division One assured, Blues manager Peter Taylor decided to give Royce an extended run in the first team as he took Sansome's place for the remaining dozen games of the season. Despite the disappointment of losing his position, Sansome had enjoyed a remarkable season which had seen him overhaul Harry Threadgold's longstanding appearance record for a Blues custodian.

The 1995/96 season proved a personal disappointment for Sansome as Royce played every match of the campaign, although the youngster's excellent progress had been helped by Sansome's coaching. The following season saw him come in for four matches after Royce had a rare poor performance. Sansome's unswerving loyalty was rewarded in July 1997 with a testimonial match against Millwall. He had already parted company with the Blues by this stage and joined Steve Lovell, as player-coach of Gravesend & Northfleet. His stint at Stonebridge Road turned out to be brief and Sansome subsequently left the game to set up his own tool-hire business.

Jimmy Shankly
Striker

Born: Glenbuck, Strathclyde, 19/6/1902

Died: 1972

Joined: June 1928, from Sheffield Utd

First team debut: v. Bournemouth, 25/8/28

Appearances: 152

Goals: 100

Other clubs: Carlisle Utd, 1922-26 & 1935-36; Sheffield Utd, 1926-28; Barrow, 1933-35

Shankly first played for Carlisle, but then signed for Sheffield United in 1926. In his first season, he was unable to gain a regular first-team place, due to the form of Johnson, Gillespie and Mercer. Although Johnson was on his way to becoming United's all-time record goalscorer, Shankly replaced him in five matches and performed well, scoring four goals. In 1927/28, despite the team's erratic form, Johnson was even more prolific, scoring 43 goals in 44 matches, restricting Shankly to three games.

Shankly felt his career would be best served with a move away from Bramall Lane. In the summer of 1928, Ted Birnie chose the well-built Shankly to spearhead his forward line for the 1928/29 season. The striker set about the task in impressive fashion, scoring twice on his League debut. He formed a devastating partnership with Dickie Donoven and Jack Bailey, the three forwards scoring 60 of Southend's 80 goals that season. Shankly himself notched up 35 goals, which remains the club's record individual total for a season. His total included two hat-tricks and no less than six braces.

The 1929/30 season saw Shankly beset by injury. He managed 9 goals in 17 games but, remarkably, all his goals came in just two matches. In February 1930, he scored four in a 5-2 victory at QPR and a month later he hit five in a 6-0 demolition of Merthyr Town. The 1930/31 campaign saw Shankly remain injury free as he regained the top scorer's slot with 28 goals. His final two seasons at The Kursaal were interspersed with spells on the sidelines with various injuries. He was again top scorer for a third time during 1931/32, but spent most of the following season out injured. Shankly's second goal against Luton in April 1933 meant he was the first Southend player to reach the 100-goal figure, having already surpassed the club's goalscoring record of 76, held by Billy Hick.

Sadly, he was released in the summer of 1933. He returned to Cumbria with Barrow, with whom he spent two seasons before spending a final League season back at Carlisle United. Despite his prodigious goalscoring record for Southend, Shankly was never regarded as a crowd favourite. Many of the fans preferred the subtle skill and pace of Billy Hick to Shankly's barnstorming style of attack.

Whatever his problems with certain sections of the crowd, Jimmy Shankly's 35 goals in his first season at the club has only ever been seriously challenged by Sammy McCrory's 33 in 1957/58, and his 100-goal total has only been beaten by Roy Hollis and Billy Best – both of whom played considerably more games than he did. Jimmy Shankly died in 1972, aged sixty-nine, having watched his brother gain legendary status as manager of Liverpool.

Frank Sheard
Defender

Born: Spilsby, Lincolnshire, 29/1/1922

Joined: May 1946, from Leicester

First team debut: v. Walsall, 31/8/46

Appearances: 192

Goals: 1

Other clubs: Skegness Town, 1939-41; Leicester, 1941-45; Gainsborough Trinity, 1956

Spilsby-born Frank Sheard was seventeen in 1939 and, rather than join a League club, he enlisted into Services training and joined the RAF as a military police officer. As the conflict continued, Sheard played wartime matches for Leicester City and, when the hostilities had ceased, Southend manager Harry Warren persuaded the defender to sign for the club. He was, at first, unable to join Southend due to his involvement with Forces activities, but eventually signed in May 1946. He made his debut in the first game of the 1946/47 season. An uncompromising centre half, his rugged style made him popular with Blues fans, although his first campaign was spent as deputy for the regular centre-half pairing of Jackson and Montgomery.

He was a regular choice in the 1947/48 season, although injury forced him to miss a dozen games. A memorable time for Sheard came in two matches against Notts County in 1948. County's England international centre forward, Tommy Lawton, had got the better of Sheard, scoring twice, in a 2-1 win at Meadow Lane. When the sides met again at The Stadium two weeks later, Sheard was determined to master the striker. He was so effective that his adversary hardly got a kick although County were to have the last laugh when a speculative shot deflected off Sheard to hand the Magpies another 2-1 victory. Sheard played all but six matches of the 1948/49 campaign and despite the Blues finishing in a lowly eighteenth place in Division Three (South), only 46 goals were conceded by a defence marshalled by Sheard.

He played the majority of matches in the 1949/50 season, scoring his only Southend goal in a 1-0 victory over Bournemouth & Boscombe Athletic. This match typified Sheard's bravery when, early on, he sustained a badly gashed mouth. After receiving ten stitches, he refused to leave the field as it would leave his side reduced to ten men. Despite his bravery, an injury sustained in September 1950 saw him sidelined for a lot of the campaign, by which time Lawler and Stirling had forged a formidable partnership. Frank Sheard's last two seasons at the club saw him vying with Stirling to partner Lawler in the Blues' defence. During his Southend career, Frank Sheard gained cult status among Blues fans for his tremendous execution of the sliding tackle, but his ability to read the game was often underestimated.

Sheard played his last game for Southend in February 1953, although he continued to play in the reserves for another three seasons. He left the club in the summer of 1956 and wound down his career with Gainsborough Trinity, in his native Lincolnshire. Frank Sheard will be remembered as one of the toughest men ever to play for Southend United.

Albert 'Joe' Sibley
Striker

Born: Southend-on-Sea, Essex, 6/10/1919

Joined: August 1937, from juniors*

First team debut: v. Ipswich, 12/9/46

Appearances: 226

Goals: 44

Other clubs: Newcastle, 1947-50

Albert 'Joe' Sibley was born in Southend and represented Essex at schoolboy level. He also played for local side, Anglo Sports. From there, Sibley joined Athenian League side Barking Town and also made a few appearances as an amateur in Arsenal's 'A' team. At this time, Southend United was managed by David Jack and his father, Bob, was chief scout. Jack senior was legendary for his adroitness in spotting talent and, in 1938, he was bowled over by Barking Town's young outside forward. Sibley signed for Southend in May 1938 and played in the three Third Division (South) matches of the abandoned 1939/40 campaign, but his fledgling career was halted by the outbreak of war. During the hostilities, Sibley guested for several London clubs. During his Forces training, he was picked to represent the RAF on numerous occasions. He then enlisted in the Army and served his country in Nigeria, again being selected for representative matches.

When the war was over, Sibley rejoined Southend and starred in the first post-war season of 1946/47. Many of Cyril Thompson's 27 goals that campaign came from Sibley's accurate crossing – it is interesting that after Sibley left in February 1947, Thompson scored only six more goals. Newcastle were one of several clubs keeping an eye on Sibley's progress and signed him for £6,500.

Sibley spent three seasons on Tyneside, but was never able to gain a regular first-team place. However, he did play well for the reserves and was highly regarded. In the summer of 1950, Harry Warren offered Sibley the chance to return to Southend, which he duly accepted. Sibley slotted back into the team as if he had never been away. Save for the odd injury, Joe Sibley became a fixture at outside right for the next five seasons. He was ever-present during the 1952/53 campaign and was second in the goalscoring list behind Cyril Grant, with 10 goals. He repeated this goal tally for the next season, despite the Blues struggling to sixteenth place in Division Three (South).

By the 1955/56 campaign, he had lost his place to younger players like Crichton Lockhart and Dickie Dowsett, but his sterling service was rewarded with a testimonial match – with a joint beneficiary, Southend's long-serving trainer, Bill Cartwright. The match against Ted Drake's Chelsea took place at Roots Hall in April 1956, with two of Sibley's old Blues team mates, Jack French and Joe O'Neil, augmenting the current side. Typically, Sibley played so well that he was picked for the final Football League match of the season against Torquay. His only appearance of the 1955/56 season proved a fitting swansong for a much loved player, who retired during the summer of 1956.

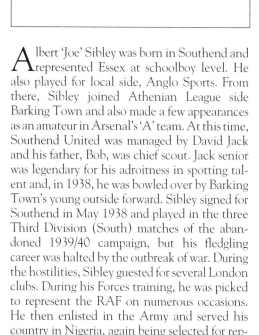

Peter Silvester
Striker

Born: Wokingham, Buckinghamshire, 19/2/1948

Joined: February 1974, from Norwich

First team debut: v. Aldershot, 16/2/74

Appearances: 89(2)

Goals: 37

Other clubs: Reading, 1965-69; Norwich, 1969-73; Baltimore Comets (USA), 1974-75; San Diego Jaws (USA), 1976; Vancouver Whitecaps (Canada), 1976; Washington Diplomats (USA), 1977; Cambridge Utd, 1977-78

Peter had trials for both Chelsea and Reading at the age of fifteen. Reading took the plunge and signed him – which was too bad for Chelsea, who came back with an offer after the signing had taken place. Having progressed through the ranks at Elm Park, Peter made his first-team debut in April 1967, but managed only a handful of appearances that season, before becoming a first-team regular in 1968/69, scoring 18 goals.

In September 1969, Peter transferred to Norwich City, and notched 10 goals in his first season. His second season proved even more fruitful, scoring 15 goals and helping Norwich City to promotion from the Second to the First Division. Everything was going well and Peter had scored 12 goals by Christmas when disaster struck. An injury led to a leg operation and Peter was sidelined for a year. Unfortunately, after returning from the operation, Peter suffered another year of niggling injuries, and it wasn't until the start of the 1973/74 season that he reached full fitness again. By this time, the Norwich manager John Bond had signed Ted McDougall and Phil Boyer, and, realising that his first-team opportunities would be limited, Peter took a gamble and dropped to the Third Division, joining Southend in February 1974.

Peter scored on his debut and he finished the 1973/74 season with 6 goals in 17 League matches. The following season saw him flitting in and out of the team, making 26 appearances and scoring 8 goals, before he really hit form in the 1975/76 season – 23 goals in 47 matches was an incredible return for a team that finished next-to-bottom in the Third Division, suffering relegation to the basement division. After only one appearance the following season, Peter left Southend United to join the exodus of talent that was moving across the ocean to America, joining the Baltimore Comets.

In 18 appearances in his first season, Peter ended as the League's second highest scorer with 14 goals. The following season, 1975, he scored only 5 goals in 19 games, and the Comets finished bottom of their division. Peter was with the San Diego Jaws in 1976, but could not rediscover that touch in front of goal, only managing 4 in 13 games for a team who finished bottom of the Pacific Conference Southern Division. Peter left San Diego before the end of the campaign, joining the Vancouver Whitecaps in July 1976, but he couldn't help them progress further than the first round of the play-offs.

Peter's tour of the States ended in 1977, after a season with the Washington Diplomats in which only 3 goals in 12 matches persuaded him it was time to return to England. He returned in August 1977, joining Cambridge United, but this was short-lived and he retired from League action in 1977 at the age of twenty-nine.

Andy Smillie
Striker/Midfielder

Born: Ilford, Essex, 15/3/1941

Joined: September 1964, from Scunthorpe

First team debut: v. Watford, 3/10/1964

Appearances: 180

Goals: 29

Other clubs: West Ham, 1958-61; Crystal Palace, 1961-63; Scunthorpe, 1963-64; Gillingham, 1968-71

An extremely talented inside left, Andy Smillie was also employed at left half and on the wing during his eventful time with the Blues. A gifted schoolboy footballer, he was taken on as a junior by West Ham and, while with them, gained England Youth caps. He turned professional in August 1958 and, although never becoming a regular at Upton Park, he performed well when called upon.

In the summer of 1961, Ted Fenton reluctantly allowed him to leave for Crystal Palace. Smillie enjoyed two successful seasons at Selhurst Park and found goals easy to come by, scoring 23 times during his time with the Eagles. In July 1963, he took a surprise move to Second Division Scunthorpe United. However, after a couple of months, Scunthorpe were struggling at the bottom of the table and Smillie and his family had failed to settle in the north.

In late September 1964, with his old West Ham mentor, Ted Fenton, now in charge at Roots Hall, Southend offered Smillie a return to the south. Fenton had been having problems filling the inside-left berth during the early matches of the 1964/65 campaign, Ashworth, Friel and Slater all failing to impress in that role. Smillie's arrival was very welcome and he went straight into the side, supporting Smith, Gilfillan and McKinven in the Southend attack. Smillie scored his first Blues goal in a dramatic match at

Roots Hall, which saw Southend defeat Bristol Rovers 6-3. Although the club would finish the season in mid-table, Smillie contributed a worthy tally of 9 goals.

The 1965/66 season saw Southend with a new manager, Alvan Williams, but the campaign was an unmitigated disaster – the Blues suffering their first ever relegation. Smillie played in all but three matches, including the club's record League defeat – 1-9 at Brighton – in November 1965. Smillie's endeavour was rewarded when Ernie Shepherd was promoted to manager in April 1967, following Williams' resignation. Shepherd immediately installed Smillie as club captain. The move almost paid dividends in the 1967/68 season when Shepherd, with Smillie as his on-the-field voice, took Southend to within four points of a return to the Third Division. However, the following campaign was to be Smillie's last at Roots Hall and he was transferred to Gillingham in October 1968.

Smillie served the Gills for three seasons and, despite surviving a couple of near misses, he could not prevent his side from getting relegated to the Fourth Division at the end of the 1970/71 campaign. He was released during the summer of 1971 and left the professional game at the relatively young age of thirty. He returned to Southend and has run a seafront restaurant for many years.

Alf Smirk

Striker

Born: Pershore, West Midlands, 14/3/1917

Joined: June 1938, from Sheffield Wednesday

First team debut: v. Torquay, 31/8/38

Appearances: 114

Goals: 32

Other clubs: Sheffield Wednesday, 1935-37; Sunderland Bus Company, 1937-38; Gateshead, 1947-48

Alf Smirk was born in Worcestershire and was awarded an England schoolboy cap in 1931. In January 1935, he signed professional forms with Sheffield Wednesday – who were a formidable First Division side at the time and won the FA Cup in April 1935. Smirk progressed well under Billy Walker's watchful eye, but when Walker left in 1937, Smirk was one of several players released by new manager, Jimmy McMullen. At first, Smirk was reduced to playing in amateur matches for the Sunderland Bus Company. However, on the recommendation of his father (and chief scout), Southend manager David Jack took a look at Smirk. As he was looking to strengthen his squad for the 1938/39 season, Smirk was offered a contract.

Smirk made the best possible start, scoring the Blues' goal in a 1-1 draw against Torquay in August 1938. He played in all the remaining fixtures of that campaign, including the three epic FA Cup third round matches against Chesterfield. The first match at Saltergate had been abandoned due to dense fog, and when the match was restaged a 1-1 draw ensued on a frozen, snow-covered pitch. The replay at The Stadium was a titanic encounter, which was all square at 2-2 after ninety minutes. Sid Bell quickly scored twice in extra time before Chesterfield pulled one back with a hotly disputed penalty. As extra time wound down, the referee penalised Southend 'keeper George McKenzie for retaliation and astonishingly awarded the Spireites a second penalty. All hell broke loose as the Southend players harangued the officials and the supporters bayed for blood. Len Bolan was ordered from the field and McKenzie saved the spot kick. Alf Smirk, as well as team mates Bolan and Bell, were charged with disorderly behaviour by the FA, Smirk being fined and warned about his future conduct.

The outbreak of war curtailed normal football activities, although Smirk played in many wartime matches for the Blues. Having missed out on six years of his career, Smirk signed on again with Southend when the first official post-war season started in 1946. He was Southend's only ever present and contributed 12 goals, being one of four Blues marksmen to attain double figures that term. The 1947/48 season saw Smirk struggling to hold a regular place and he felt his days at The Stadium were numbered.

In March 1948, he joined Gateshead. After only 11 games, Smirk retired from the professional game. He joined Chingford, and was later player-manager of Loughborough-based Brush Sports. On retiring from the game he became a journalist and, often, a critic of the Blues during spells with the *Southend Times* and *Southend Standard*. Alf Smirk was still living in the area when he died in 1996, aged seventy-nine.

Dave Smith
Manager

Born: Dundee, Tayside, 22/9/1933

Joined: May 1976, as manager

Other clubs: Burnley, 1950-51;
Brighton & Hove Albion, 1961-62;
Bristol City, 1962-63

Dave Smith is arguably the most popular and charismatic manager in the club's history. As a player, Smith hardly excelled, having started as a youngster with Burnley. He spent eleven seasons at Turf Moor, but made less than 100 League appearances – although his progress was hampered by injury problems. Remarkably, during his playing career, Smith broke his leg on no less than five occasions. At the end of the 1960/61 season, he was given a free transfer by Clarets manager, Harry Potts, whose man management and motivational skills inspired Smith in his own management career.

In July 1961, Smith joined Brighton but could not establish a regular place in the side. At the age of thirty, his injury-ravaged playing career ended with a brief spell at Bristol City. He then became a successful coach at Sheffield Wednesday followed by Newcastle. In the early 1970s, Smith became reserve-team manager at Arsenal, before taking his first managerial job at Mansfield in 1974. In his inaugural season, he took the Stags to the Fourth Division title and the quarter-final of the League Cup.

In May 1976, he took over as Southend manager. In his second season at Roots Hall, he guided the Blues back to the Third Division. However, with his side suffering a goalscoring crisis, the club were relegated at the end of the 1979/80 season and the Blues chairman warned

that promotion was required if Smith was to remain in the job. The Scot duly signed two new strikers, Mercer and Spence. They were to prove to be the pieces that had been missing from the Smith masterplan. A cast iron defence was augmented with Smith's persistence in the use of wingers. The new line-up was sensational as the Blues won the Fourth Division, shattering many club records.

Progress was maintained during 1981/82, but the following season the club's owners, the Rubins, sold the club to businessman Anton Johnson and Smith was sacked by telegram whilst on holiday. He returned to Roots Hall, staged a sit-in protest and successfully sued the club for wrongful dismissal. Following his departure, Southend suffered some of its darkest days, culminating in near bankruptcy in 1985.

Smith went on to manage Plymouth Argyle and guided the club to within three points of the play-offs for a First Division place in 1986/87. In the 1987/88 season, he briefly managed Dundee. He left the game for a while, before returning to Devon in 1989 to manage Torquay for two seasons. Dave Smith was an inspirational manager who could be tough-talking but understanding when it came to his players' needs. His love of football was always evident and he is still remembered fondly by all the Blues fans who witnessed his exciting teams in full flight.

Ray Smith
Striker

Born: Islington, North London, 18/4/1943

Joined: December 1961, from Basildon

First team debut: v. Newport County, 10/2/62

Appearances: 162

Goals: 57

Other clubs: Basildon Town, 1959-61; Wrexham, 1967-72; Peterborough, 1972-73

Ray Smith's career took off as a teenager with Basildon Town, and in the 1960/61 season Smith scored prolifically in the Basildon & District League. His goalscoring garnered publicity in the *Southend Standard*, and, after viewing the young forward for himself, Ted Fenton signed him for the Blues in December 1961.

Smith was still a raw eighteen-year-old and, after a few games in the reserves, Fenton brought him into the first team in February 1962. Smith was unlucky not to score on his debut against Newport, but found the net in his third game, a 3-1 triumph at Watford. The youngster was hoping to gain a regular place in the starting eleven for the 1962/63 season, but with Jones, Beesley and McKinven all contributing double-figure goal tallies, Smith often found himself on the sidelines. When he did get a chance, he played well, scoring 8 goals in only 15 starts. The following campaign saw Smith facing even stiffer competition for a place, following the arrival of Bobby Gilfillan and Jimmy Conway. However, Smith did feature more prominently and his total of 12 for the season was only one behind top scorer Beesley. The 1964/65 campaign was to prove the last as manager for Ted Fenton and Smith was reduced to a supporting role for the prolific Gilfillan, who scored 23 goals. New manager Alvan Williams took an instant shine to

the well-built forward, and Smith was picked for all but five matches during the 1965/66 season. Fortunately for Smith, one of his few absences of that campaign was the humiliating 1-9 reversal at Brighton, Southend's record League defeat.

He provided an excellent foil for Firmani and learned a lot from the former Italian international. However, the team had a disastrous season and suffered their first relegation. Ray Smith's most memorable campaign for the Blues came in 1966/67, when he top scored with 19 goals. He hit his first hat-trick for the club in a 5-1 victory against Chester and repeated the feat in a 4-0 defeat of Bradford Park Avenue. However, by April 1967, Alvan Williams, having promised an instant return to the Third Division, jumped ship to join Wrexham. Williams returned to Roots Hall in the summer to plunder Eddie May and Ray Smith.

Smith was at The Racecourse Ground for a considerably longer time than Williams, who was forced to resign within a year after a drink-driving charge. Smith went on to become a huge favourite with the Welsh club, scoring 60 goals in five seasons. Smith then joined Peterborough United in July 1972, but after an unimpressive spell at London Road, Noel Cantwell released him at the end of that campaign. He returned to North Wales with Bangor City, where he saw out his playing days. Since then, he has worked for Firestones in Wrexham.

Derek Spence
Striker

Born: Belfast, 18/1/1952

Joined: December 1979, from Blackpool

First team debut: v. Rotherham, 12/1/80

Appearances: 109(4)

Goals: 34

Other clubs: Crusaders (N. Ireland), 1968-70; Oldham Athletic, 1970-73; Bury, 1973-76 & 1983-84; Blackpool, 1976-77 & 1978-79; Olympiakos Pireaus (Greece), 1977-78; See Bee (Hong Kong), 1982-83

Derek Spence's playing career started in Belfast, with the Crusaders club, before he joined Oldham in December 1970. However, the form of David Shaw and Jim Fryatt, meant Spence had to wait until April 1972 for his League debut. He failed to impress Oldham manager Jimmy Frizzell and was consigned to the reserves until he moved to Bury in February 1973. At Gigg Lane, Spence soon found his scoring touch, netting in two of his first three games.

The 1973/74 campaign saw Spence miss only two League games and he was top scorer with 16 goals, as Bury were promoted to the Third Division. As the Shakers consolidated their status, Spence became an idol, scoring nearly 50 League goals in three seasons. He also became a full international for Northern Ireland, making his debut in April 1975. It was a very unpopular move when, in October 1976, Bury manager Bobby Smith sold Spence to Blackpool – the move coming a day after Spence had scored his first international goal in a 2-2 draw against Holland in Rotterdam.

His goalscoring touch deserted him at Bloomfield Road – although this was not helped by the manager's decision to play him in a wide role, supporting the two main strikers. After a disappointing season, Spence was offered a move to Olympiakos of Pireaus. The Greek side were going through a lean spell, however, and Spence returned to Blackpool at the end of the 1977/78 season. His second spell at Blackpool was more productive, and he finished the season as top scorer with 16 goals. At Southend, Dave Smith realised his strike force of Parker and Tuohy was not working as the Blues were struggling in the Third Division.

In January 1980, Smith prised Spence away from Bloomfield Road. A month later, Parker was sold and Spence had a new partner as Mercer arrived from Watford. Although the acquisitions of Spence and Mercer did not prevent the Blues suffering relegation, the two forwards were to play a pivotal part in the club's history. In the 1980/81 season, both players scored hatfuls of goals as Southend won their first major trophy, the Fourth Division championship. Spence top scored with 21 goals and he was justly rewarded with the Player of the Year trophy.

The Blues pushed hard all season during the 1981/82 campaign, but six straight draws spoilt the club's chances of promotion. Spence's scoring touch had deserted him, with the burden of getting the goals falling to Mercer and Steve Phillips. Spence felt in need of a fresh challenge and in the summer of 1982 he flew out to Hong Kong for a season with See Bee. He returned to Bury for a second spell in 1983, but could not recapture past glories. Spence wound down his career with Rossendale United.

111

Micky Stead

Defender

Born: West Ham, East London, 28/2/1957

Joined: September 1978, from Tottenham

First team debut: v. Sheffield Wednesday, 9/9/78

Appearances: 340(1)

Goals: 5

Other clubs: Tottenham, 1973-78; Doncaster Rovers, 1985-87

Micky Stead was born in West Ham in 1957 but was overlooked by his local club and joined Tottenham as an apprentice in July 1973. During the 1973/74 season, Micky won an FA Youth Cup winners medal as Tottenham, having defeated archrivals Arsenal in the semi-final, beat Huddersfield Town 2-1 on aggregate in the two-legged final.

Micky signed professional forms in November 1974, making his first-team debut in February 1976. A year later, Stead spent a month on loan to Swansea, during which time he scored his first senior goal, against Aldershot. On returning to White Hart Lane, with Naylor and Holmes cemented in the full-back roles, Stead soon realised his first-team chances would be limited. He moved to Roots Hall, initially on loan, but impressing enough to persuade Dave Smith to sign him permanently. Starting his Blues career as a right-back, Micky soon became a fixture in the Southend United team. He made 43 appearances for the club in the 1978/79 season, including both matches against Liverpool in the FA Cup – games he describes as the most memorable of his career.

The 1979/80 campaign was a disappointing one for the club, culminating in relegation, but Micky excelled in a new midfield role, playing all but four of the club's matches that season. He even managed 2 goals in that campaign. The 1980/81 season was Southend's championship-winning campaign, and Micky reverted to his no-nonsense, tough-tackling full-back role. This season, and the next one, saw one of the most dominant defensive lines in the club's history, with Stead, Yates, Moody and Cusack proving very hard to breach.

The 1982/83 season saw Micky miss only one game. Although Southend found themselves relegated at the end of the 1983/84 campaign, Micky won the Player of the Year award for his admirable efforts during a dismal season. He played 38 games of the disastrous 1984/85 campaign, when the Blues narrowly avoided the ignominy of applying for re-election to the League. Stead started the 1985/86 campaign as the only survivor of the title-winning team and marshalled a back line that included Frank Lampard, as well as Steve Hatter and Shane Westley. In November 1985, having received a warm ovation from a Roots Hall crowd, Micky decided to leave for pastures new, moving north to join Doncaster Rovers, who were then managed by former team mate Dave Cusack.

After 83 League games at Belle Vue, Micky left League football, returning to London with Fisher Athletic, for whom he would later become joint manager. A great servant and consistent performer, Micky sits at ninth in the all-time list of most appearances made in a Southend shirt.

Jimmy Stirling
Defender

Born: Airdrie, Strathclyde, 23/6/1925

Joined: December 1950, from Birmingham

First team debut: v. Port Vale, 2/12/50

Appearances: 233

Goals: 2

Other clubs: Coltness, 1943-47; Bournemouth, 1947-50; Birmingham, 1950-51; Poole Town, 1960-62

After playing for Coltness United, Jimmy joined Bournemouth in July 1947, having served in the Army with the Scots Guard. After nearly three years with the Cherries, in which he made 73 League appearances, scored one goal and ended up as captain, Jimmy transferred to Birmingham City in June 1950.

After only six months in the Midlands, Jimmy realised he would not be able to break into the first team at St Andrews, and transferred to Southend in December 1950. Jimmy made his debut for the Blues in December 1950, going on to make 26 appearances in his first season. The following campaign saw Frank Sheard win the tussle for the number five shirt, leaving Jimmy with only 10 League appearances. They struggled for supremacy again in the 1952/53 season, both men almost equally sharing the available games. With Frank Sheard leaving the club at the end of the 1952/53 season, Jimmy must have felt he had the shirt to himself, but didn't reckon on Bill Pavitt, who started the season as first choice, before Jimmy edged him out.

The beginning and end of the 1954/55 season had Jimmy in the first team, including an appearance in the final match at The Stadium, but he actually only made 9 first-team starts that campaign, due to the exceptional form of Denis Howe. The following season began with Denis Howe playing in the opening 21 League matches, but Jimmy finally dislodged him in December, going on to make 25 League appearances and 2 FA Cup starts – including the famous Manchester City home defeat. The 1956/57 season was the best of Jimmy's Blues career so far, with 41 first-team appearances, including memorable cup games against Liverpool and Birmingham City. However, the 1957/58 season was particularly special, as he played in every first-team game and even registered his first Southend goal in December.

However this was to be the peak of his Blues career, and after only 19 League appearances in 1958/59, Jimmy travelled to Austria for a trial with Simmering. His visit to the outfit was reported as being 'not quite what he had been led to believe' and nothing more came of it. He returned to Roots Hall to make a single appearance in the 1959/60 season, before calling it a day. Interestingly, Jimmy was quoted in a 1959 Southend programme as being 'nothing if not versatile'. This was because 'in the summer months he can turn his hand to many tasks. During the last few years he had worked in the Kursaal fairground, in a brick-making plant, at Coryton and as a painter and decorator in Weymouth' – certainly a far cry from the pampered professionals of today! On leaving the professional game, Jimmy Stirling ran a newsagents in Bournemouth for many years.

Les Stubbs

Striker

Born: Great Wakering, Essex, 18/2/1929

Joined: May 1948, from Great Wakering Rovers*

First team debut: v. Torquay, 1/4/50

Appearances: 111

Goals: 48

Other clubs: Great Wakering Rovers, 1946-48; Chelsea, 1952-58

When Southend United beat Torquay United 4-2 at Plainmoor on April Fools Day 1950, the Southend supporters who had congregated outside the Southend Standard offices – to get news of the game as it progressed – were left asking each other 'Who is Stubbs?', as the player scored two of the four Southend goals that day. Les Stubbs was, in fact, a twenty-one-year-old inside forward who had signed for the Blues from local amateur side Great Wakering Rovers in May 1948. He had been nursed through the youth ranks by the club, and was only on the Easter trips to Newport County and Torquay United on educational grounds. However, Harry Warren suddenly found himself short of forwards when Freddie Morris picked up an injury in the 2-1 defeat at Somerton Park. He only had Stubbs to call on and decided to throw him in at the deep end. Stubbs responded well with two goals and another in the next game, a 2-2 home draw against Ipswich Town

Despite this auspicious start, Stubbs did not become a regular first-team player until halfway through the 1950/51 campaign, but made up for lost time by rattling in 19 goals in only 31 matches. He ended the season as top scorer,

being four ahead of Albert Wakefield, and managed to score braces on no less than five occasions. The following campaign he scored 18 in 36 appearances, leaving him level with Cyril Grant's total, although this time beaten by Wakefield's 21 League and cup goals. Stubbs was also selected for an England 'B' Trial XI, scoring against the British Olympic XI at Highbury Stadium. By now, his form was attracting the attention of the bigger clubs, and he joined First Division Chelsea in November 1952.

He stayed at Stamford Bridge for six years, and in the 1954/55 season he made 28 appearances and scored 5 goals as Chelsea became First Division champions, finishing four points ahead of second-placed Wolves. Although never truly a regular for Chelsea, Stubbs made 112 appearances, netting 34 goals, and was regarded as a hardworking, honest professional by his manager, legendary goalscorer Ted Drake. Stubbs rejoined Southend in November 1958, but unfortunately for the club and Les himself, he was unable to recapture his form of old. Southend already boasted prolific forwards, such as Roy Hollis, Sammy McCrory and Bud Houghton – who were all scoring on a regular basis – so, after only 23 games and 3 goals, Les Stubbs left the Blues in July 1960. He signed for Southern League Bedford Town, where he finished his playing career.

Peter Taylor
Striker

Born: Southend-on-Sea, Essex, 3/1/1953

Joined: January 1971, from apprentice

First team debut: v. Barrow, 6/11/70

Appearances: 59(19)

Goals: 13

Other clubs: Crystal Palace, 1973-76; Tottenham, 1976-80; Leyton Orient, 1980-82; Maidstone Utd, 1983 & 1984-86; Exeter, 1983-84; Heybridge Swifts, 1986-87; Chelmsford, 1987-88

Peter Taylor was one of the most talented footballers to emerge from the Southend area. He first came to the fore playing at schoolboy level for Canvey Island. In 1970, he was offered an apprenticeship at Roots Hall and made rapid progress. In November of that year, Southend manager Arthur Rowley had no hesitation in handing the eighteen-year-old Taylor, who had earned the nickname 'Spud', a first-team debut for the home game against Barrow. Taylor was still on apprentice forms, but his enormous potential was recognised with the offer of a professional contract in January 1971.

He played a handful of matches in the remainder of that season. In the summer of 1971 he was the star player in two youth tournaments won by Southend United. In one match in Germany, he scored four goals in a 6-0 victory against TSV Trebur. The 1971/72 season was a bit of a disappointment, as Taylor was often used as a substitute in the first team, although he was top scorer in the reserves, netting 18 goals in the Midweek Football League. One of his substitute appearances in the first team came in strange circumstances. In the home game with Cambridge, Blues 'keeper Derek Bellotti was injured and, despite his lack of height, Taylor volunteered to go in goal – a brave effort could not prevent a 1-2 defeat, however. Taylor really made the breakthrough in the 1972/73 season, when he

made the left-wing berth his own and turned in some memorable performances. Chris Guthrie particularly benefited from his ability to deliver accurate crosses.

His obvious talent meant several clubs were casting an eye in his direction. In October 1973, Crystal Palace manager Malcolm Allison made an offer Southend couldn't refuse. The fee agreed was £120,000, which represented a new record transfer fee received by the club. Taylor made his Palace debut at Oxford and kept his place for the remainder of the season. In the 1974/75 campaign, he was Palace's top scorer, with 15 League and cup goals as Palace missed out on promotion to the Second Division by four points. He again scored well for Palace during 1975/76, netting a dozen goals, although his tally was augmented when he took over penalty duties. In the FA Cup he hit four goals as Palace progressed as far as the semi-finals, before being beaten by eventual winners Southampton.

Taylor's form with Palace was so good that, despite being a Third Division player, he was selected to play for England against Wales at Wrexham, coming on as a substitute for Mick Channon. He then played in the next three England matches against Wales, Northern Ireland and Scotland, scoring the only goal of the match against Wales in Cardiff. In September 1976 he finally gained a move to the

First Division, when Tottenham paid £200,000 for his services – a fee that would later rise to £400,000. However, Taylor found himself in a desperately poor Spurs side, who finished bottom of the First Division at the end of that season. In 1977/78, Taylor contributed 11 goals towards Tottenham's successful effort to regain their top-flight status – albeit on goal difference from fourth-place Brighton.

Taylor was again a regular for the 1978/79 season, playing alongside World Cup winners Osvaldo Ardiles and Ricardo Villa. His last two seasons at White Hart Lane saw his appearances restricted, however, and he was sold to Leyton Orient in November 1980 for £150,000. He scored on his debut for the O's, against Bristol Rovers, and hit five in his first seven matches. The 1981/82 season was a disaster for Taylor and Orient. In December, Taylor broke his ankle at Bolton and, in his absence, the O's were relegated to the Second Division. During the 1982/83 season, he became unsettled at Brisbane Road and was briefly loaned to Oldham Athletic. In March 1983, he was released and joined non-League Maidstone United as player-coach. In September 1983, he returned to the Football League with a brief spell at Exeter, but his stint there ended in acrimony, following a row which developed after the Grecians suffered

an embarrassing FA Cup defeat to, of all teams, Maidstone United. Taylor rejoined Maidstone and later played for Heybridge Swifts and Chelmsford City.

He moved into management with Dartford, before rejoining Southend as manager in December 1993, after Barry Fry had departed for Birmingham. His spell in the Roots Hall hotseat was inglorious, as the club struggled to survive in Division One. The fans that once cheered him as a player hounded him as a manager and, following three straight defeats in February 1995, he offered his resignation. He resurfaced as manager of Conference outfit Dover Athletic, but when his old Spurs team mate Glenn Hoddle took the England job, Taylor was surprisingly offered the job of under-21 manager. He was a tremendous success, the side were unbeaten during his time in charge and there was widespread media criticism when the FA revealed his contract would not be renewed.

He was managing Gillingham when the Leicester City manager's job became vacant, following Martin O'Neill's departure to Celtic, and Taylor found himself in charge of a Premiership club. After a promising start, his tenure at Filbert Street turned sour and he was dismissed a few weeks into the 2001/02 season. However, Taylor soon took up the manager's job at Brighton.

Cyril Thompson
Striker

Born: Southend-on-Sea, Essex, 18/12/1918

Joined: August 1945, from local football

First team debut: v. Watford. 11/11/45

Appearances: 70

Goals: 41

Other clubs: Derby County, 1948-50; Brighton & Hove Albion; 1950-51; Watford, 1951-53

Cyril Thompson was a prominent local amateur player when the Second World War broke out. During the war, emergency competitions were organised to help raise public morale. In the 1945/46 season, Southend were placed in the Third Division South (North Region), and in the second half of the campaign they competed in the Third Division (South) Cup – which had a qualifying competition based on a league system. The club drafted in many locally-based players, and Cyril Thompson impressed greatly, scoring 9 times in only 13 matches. He performed particularly well in the League Cup competition, forming a good partnership with another product from the local amateur scene, Frank Dudley.

Both men were offered professional contracts by Harry Warren and made their official debuts in the FA Cup tie against Watford in November 1945. Thompson's first goals for the Blues came in the famous 'Hankey' match at Eastville against Bristol Rovers in October 1946, when he scored twice in a 3-1 victory. He followed this with a hat-trick at Norwich a month later, finishing the season as the club's leading scorer with 27 League and cup goals – eleven ahead of Dudley and Harry Lane. The 1947/48 season saw Southend in less prolific form, especially away from home, the team managing only 51 goals – Thompson keeping his top scorer's crown with

14. An injury sustained at Norwich in April 1948, saw him miss the last three games of that season. The match at Carrow Road was to prove Thompson's last for the Blues, as in July 1948 he joined First Division Derby County for £5,000.

Derby's manager, Stuart McMillan, showed great faith in the inexperienced Thompson and played him in the first twelve First Division fixtures of the 1948/49 campaign. Thompson's return of three goals was deemed insufficient and he lost his place to Jack Stamps. He would appear in only two more matches that season and, after playing at half-back in his only two appearances of the 1949/50 campaign, his days at the Baseball Ground were numbered. In March 1951, he was released to join Brighton & Hove Albion, who were in the Third Division (South). He stayed at the Goldstone Ground for a year and rediscovered his touch in front of goal. In March 1952, he moved to Watford, two seasons at Vicarage Road yielding a useful return of 36 goals.

Thompson retired at the end of the 1953/54 season at the age of thirty-five. Like many of his generation, he lost six years of his playing career due to the war, but his brief spell at Southend saw a prolific burst of goalscoring that makes him worthy of inclusion as one of the club's greats.

Harry Threadgold
Goalkeeper

Born: Tattenhall, Cheshire, 6/11/1924

Died: 1996

Joined: June 1953, from Sunderland

First team debut: v. Norwich, 19/8/53

Appearances: 343

Goals: 0

Other clubs: Tarvin Utd, 1945-47; Chester, 1947-52; Sunderland, 1952-53

Harry Threadgold served in the Marines in the Second World War, and it was during the hostilities he became recognised as one of the Forces' best boxers. After Threadgold demobilised, he started playing for amateur side Tarvin United in the Chester & District League. He starred as a goalkeeper at that level and was soon offered professional terms at Chester, who were in the Third Division (North). He played under Frank Brown at Sealand Road for two seasons and, despite the team struggling in the lower reaches of the division, he progressed sufficiently to earn a move to First Division Sunderland.

Threadgold played the majority of League games in the 1952/53 season, but Sunderland boss Bill Murray surprisingly allowed him to join Southend in the summer of 1953. He immediately took over first-team goalkeeping duties from Irish international Tommy Scannell and played in all but four games in his first season with the club. The next four campaigns saw Threadgold miss few matches and he kept goal in some memorable FA Cup encounters, against the likes of Everton, Manchester City and Birmingham during that period. The 1958/59 season saw Threadgold suffer a spate of injuries, usually due to his extreme bravery when diving at the feet of onrushing forwards. He played only half the games that season, with Brian Ronson deputising in his enforced absence.

It was around this time that Threadgold discovered his dislike for playing football under floodlights. He blamed the glare from the early type of bulbs used for some below-par performances. Threadgold's reluctance to play in floodlit games posed a problem for Southend manager Eddie Perry, who responded by signing Peter Goy from Arsenal in October 1960. Threadgold's last three seasons with Southend were spent in competition with Goy and, although he missed many matches, he did manage to exceed Billy Moore's longstanding League appearance record for a Southend goalkeeper – playing in his 305th game for the Blues at Notts County in April 1962. His new record would remain unbeaten for more than thirty years, until Paul Sansome set the present record.

Threadgold's ten seasons at the club saw him gain enormous popularity among supporters and, in recognition of his bravery and loyalty, the club arranged two benefit matches for him in 1958 – against Leyton Orient and Brighton, when Jimmy Duthie and Doug Young were co-beneficiaries. He retired at the end of the 1962/63 season and became landlord of the Ship Hotel in Leigh until his retirement. Harry Threadgold died in 1996 at the age of seventy-one, although his son, John, kept the Threadgold name associated with the club, being Southend's kit man in the late 1990s.

Steve Tilson
Midfielder

Born: Wickford, Essex, 27/7/1966

Joined: February 1989, from Witham Town

First team debut: v. Mansfield, 11/2/89

Appearances: 225(43)

Goals: 31

Other clubs: Basildon, 1984-86; Bowers Utd, 1986-87; Witham Town, 1986-89; Canvey Island, 1997-2001

When Southend United supporters were asked to nominate their Player of the Millennium, they could have gone for many famous names – for example, Collymore, Cadette, Best or Crown – but the player chosen was local boy Steve Tilson. The midfielder from Wickford almost missed his chance in the professional game, having left Bromfords School in 1982 without attracting any attention from Football League clubs. He took a job working on a building site for a local firm, Curnicks, and at weekends would play for various Essex Senior League sides. He started with Basildon United, moving on to near neighbours Bowers United, before a move to Witham Town that changed his football career.

Since he was a youngster, Steve had followed Southend and always harboured an ambition to pull on the blue shirt of the Shrimpers. His manager at Witham was a former Blues player, Danny Greaves (the son of the legendary England forward, Jimmy). Greaves was hugely impressed with the subtle midfield skills of Tilson, and it was patently obvious that he could play at a much higher level. Greaves finally persuaded Southend manager Dave Webb to give Tilson a trial in a reserve fixture. Webb was sufficiently impressed to offer him a contract on the spot.

Although he would be earning less than he received for his building job, Tilson jumped at the chance – not only did it fulfil a boyhood dream but, at twenty-two, he felt time was passing him by if he was going to make a career in football. Tilson made his first-team debut as a substitute in a 0-4 defeat at Mansfield in February 1989 and scored his first goal a month later in a victory over Wolves.

He made the left-side midfield position his own during the 1990/91 Third Division campaign, which saw the Blues narrowly miss out on the championship by one point from Cambridge United. Tilson was one of five players to contribute a double-figure tally of goals in that memorable season and his haul of 11 included a hat-trick in the 10-1 demolition of Aldershot in the Leyland DAF Cup. Southend's first-ever Division Two campaign saw Tilson play in every match for the club, but the 1992/93 campaign, under the management of Colin Murphy, saw him initially lose his place to new signing Kevin O'Callaghan. However, worse was to follow under Barry Fry the following season, when he was almost totally overlooked, starting just 3 Division

Tilson is pictured on the right.

One matches all season. In September 1993, he was loaned briefly to Brentford.

When Peter Taylor took over as manager, following Fry's moonlight flit to Birmingham, Tilson was restored to the side, Taylor seeing him as a younger version of himself. The 1995/96 season saw Ronnie Whelan installed as manager and Tilson figured in just over half the League matches. In January 1997, Tilson suffered his first serious injury during his time at the club, picking up a hernia in a match at Port Vale that would see him sidelined for three months. At the end of Tilson's ninth season with the Blues, he was looking forward to a well-deserved testimonial year. However, Ronnie Whelan told him, out of the blue, that his services were no longer required as part of a wage-cutting exercise. Tilson was devastated and rightly upset – as he was one of the lowest paid players at the club. His good name

brought in offers from several other teams, including Leyton Orient and Lincoln City, but 'Tilly' publicly stated that he only really wanted to play for Southend.

Steve eventually accepted Jeff King's offer to join a growing contingent of former Shrimpers at Ryman League Canvey Island. He successfully skippered the Gulls to two straight promotions and, in four seasons at Park Lane, he has contributed over 100 goals in Canvey's remarkable rise up the non-League pyramid. In 1999, he rejoined Southend United as director of the club's successful youth academy. His playing career continued to bloom, leading Canvey to FA Trophy victory at Villa Park against Forest Green Rovers in May 2001. Steve Tilson's universal popularity can be gauged by the fact that the then chairman's shabby treatment of such a loyal club servant still rankles among Southend supporters.

Neil Townsend
Centre-half

Born: Long Buckby, Northants, 1/2/1950

Joined: July 1973, from Northampton

First team debut: v. Blackburn Rovers, 25/8/73

Appearances: 177(1)

Goals: 8

Other clubs: Northampton, 1968-72; Bedford, 1972-73; Weymouth, 1978-79; Bournemouth, 1979-81

Centre-half Neil joined Southend United from non-League Bedford Town in June 1973 for £5,000. He had been a professional player since 1968, when he signed for his local League club, Northampton Town, who had seen him make England youth international appearances against Scotland, Wales and Northern Ireland in the year that he turned professional.

Townsend made his first-team debut for Northampton in a 2-0 victory at Mansfield in November 1968. Despite making over 70 appearances for the Cobblers, he never won a regular place in the side, being mainly used when others were injured or suspended. Frustrated by his failure to establish himself at the County Ground, Townsend found himself in dispute with Cobbler's boss Dave Bowen, who first loaned and then transferred Townsend to Bedford Town. It was from the Southern League side that Arthur Rowley snapped him up in July 1973.

Neil formed a tremendous partnership with Alan Moody whilst at Southend, but the 1975/76 season was a horrendous one for him, with injuries being sustained throughout the campaign. A pre-season cracked rib kept him out of the first four matches, and on his return to the side he managed only twelve games before breaking his wrist

against Ilford on an icy pitch in the Essex Professional Cup. Neil quickly got over this setback, missing only three games before returning for two matches – a short run that ended with him being stretchered off with a badly twisted ankle against Rotherham United. Neil again returned quickly, missing only one match this time, but his comeback, a January FA Cup tie against Cardiff City, was marred by a torn groin muscle, an injury which this time kept him out for the rest of the season.

Neil played over 150 first-team matches for the Shrimpers, before moving to the South Coast with Weymouth. He wasn't in non-League football for long before Bournemouth snapped him up, and he made 34 further appearances before his League career came to an end. The type of centre half that all lower division teams look for, Neil's wholehearted attitude and aerial ability made him a favourite at Roots Hall during his five-year stay there.

Albert Wakefield

Striker

Born: Pontefract, West Yorkshire, 19/11/1921

Joined: August 1949, from Leeds

First team debut: v. Port Vale, 23/8/49

Appearances: 119

Goals: 69

Other clubs: Stanningley Works, 1939-42; Leeds, 1942-49, Clacton Town, 1953-55

Although born in Pontefract, Albert Wakefield considered Pudsey, the town of cricketers Len Hutton and Herbert Sutcliffe, to be his home. Wakefield had returned to Pudsey after serving his country in Italy during the Second World War. Strangely, his football career could have taken a completely different path, as he was offered terms by several Italian clubs. He turned them all down and started playing for Stanningley Works, from whence he joined Leeds United in October 1942.

Wakefield had to wait until the 1947/48 season to make his first-team debut at The Dell, where he scored a goal in a 2-1 Leeds victory over Southampton. A strong-running centre forward, he scored 21 goals in 37 games that season at Elland Road to finish in second place to the division's top scorer – just one goal behind Eddie Quigley of Yorkshire rivals Sheffield Wednesday. He scored a hat-trick in the last game of that personally memorable season, a 5-1 victory at home to Bury. The following campaign saw Wakefield, having scored only twice, lose his place in the side by mid-October to Len Browning, who had been promoted after scoring prolifically in the Central League side.

Wakefield transferred to Southend United for the start of the 1949/50 campaign, with part of the transfer deal seeing the Shrimpers' prolific scorer, Frank Dudley, move to Leeds for £10,000.

In four seasons with the Blues, Wakefield registered 58 League goals and a further 11 in cup matches. His cup tally included a memorable hat-trick in an FA Cup second round tie against Oldham at The Stadium in December 1951. His goals led to a 5-0 Shrimpers triumph, which was the catalyst for a run to the fifth round – where Sheffield United ended Southend's interest in the competition. Wakefield would have certainly made more appearances for the Blues, but he lost a considerable amount of playing time when he broke his leg in a match at Leyton Orient in December 1950, costing him the remainder of that campaign.

Modestly, he attributed much of his goalscoring success to the genius of Jimmy McAlinden, considering the Irishman to be the finest player he had ever played alongside. Strangely, Albert always quoted his most vivid memory in football as being the 1950 Essex Professional Cup final, a game in which the Blues defeated Leyton Orient 2-1, Wakefield scoring both goals. His final League outing was at Aldershot in February 1953 and, at the end of that season, Wakefield signed for Clacton Town, who played in the Eastern Counties League. Even now, in his late seventies, Albert Wakefield has never managed to rid himself of his love for Southend United and can still be seen on matchdays, cheering on the Blues from the East Stand at Roots Hall.

Frank Walton
Defender

Born: Southend-on-Sea, Essex, 9/4/1918

Died: 1986

Joined: August 1934, from school

First team debut: v. Cardiff, 15/1/38

Appearances: 154

Goals: 0

Other clubs: Dartford, 1951-53

Frank Walton spent almost fifty years of his life associated with Southend United Football Club. His passing in 1986 was somewhat traumatic, as most Blues supporters had never known a time at the club without his presence. Born locally, Frank joined the Shrimpers in 1937 and went on to represent them as a player, captain, director and, latterly, chairman, through the roller-coaster journey of the Blues in the lower divisions of the Football League.

An accomplished full-back, Frank represented Southend boys, as well as Essex and London boys. He then answered an appeal by Blues manager David Jack for local amateur talent and was signed immediately after his trial match. He was initially used as a winger and made his first-team debut during January 1938 in a 3-1 victory over Cardiff City. Although he made only 8 appearances before the outbreak of war, Walton's tally of 60 wartime matches for Southend was more than any other Blues player. By the time the inaugural post-war season of 1946/47 came around, he had been converted to the full-back position by new Southend manager Harry Warren – a role that he would adapt to with some aplomb.

Walton did not really establish himself as a first-team player until the 1949/50 season, when he played in every game with the exception of the last fixture at Leyton Orient. Walton had starred in the left-back position throughout a suc-cessful campaign, which resulted in the Blues finishing in third place in the Third Division (South) – only seven points adrift of the champions, Notts County. However, the 1950/51 campaign saw Walton lose his place to the emerging talent of Sandy Anderson and, in July 1951, he opted to join Southern League outfit Dartford.

Despite losing much of his career to the war, Frank made over 150 appearances for Southend, and enjoyed a benefit match against Middlesbrough in 1948. In recognition of the service he gave the club and town during his fifty-year association, his name adorns the clock above the South Stand, posthumously named in his honour when opened in 1994. It is sad that the final years of his life saw some of the darkest times in Southend's history. The club's perilous financial and playing position in the mid-1980s, coupled with the controversial Anton Johnson affair, placed Walton under considerable strain, although he always remained a kindly and approachable man.

Frank Walton always represented fans' views at boardroom level and had immense personal pride in his involvement with the club. He also remembered his roots and contributed much to local football, serving on the committee of the Southend Borough Combination – whose teams still compete for the Walton Cup.

Peter Watson
Defender

Born: Stapleford, Nottinghamshire, 15/4/1934

Joined: July 1959, from Nottingham Forest

First team debut: v. Halifax, 22/8/1959

Appearances: 263

Goals: 3

Other clubs: Nottingham Forest, 1955-59

Peter, whose younger brother Dave would go on to make 65 appearances for England, was born in Stapleford in 1934. Having played for his county as an amateur, Peter attracted the attention of Nottingham Forest, signing amateur forms with them just before starting a three-year stint in the RAF at the age of eighteen. After leaving the RAF, Peter turned professional, but in four years he managed only 13 League appearances, the brilliance of Scottish pivot Bobby McKinlay proving an immovable object. Southend manager Eddie Perry decided that Peter was the man needed to build their defence around, and he was signed in July 1959. Peter made his debut in the opening game of the 1959/60 season and missed only one game all campaign. A first goal for the Blues followed in 1960/61, in a 1-1 draw against Brentford, with another in the 1961/62 season.

Throughout this time, apart from a minor absence due to injury, Peter made the centre half position his own and it was no different in 1962/63, when he formed an excellent pairing with Terry Bradbury, helping the club to eighth in the Third Division. This partnership continued into the 1963/64 and 1964/65 seasons, the two defenders eventually appearing 111 times in Southend shirts together. Watson's value to the club was recognised by the board and they granted him a benefit match against Fulham in

April 1964. Sadly, after nearly 250 League games, a broken jaw was aggravated by another injury in a subsequent match and the combined effect led to Peter's retirement in 1966, after managing only three games in the 1965/66 season. The combination of severe injuries led to Watson suffering permanent sight problems and he realised the double vision would prevent him playing to the standard to which he had become accustomed. In November 1966, a Southend XI played an International Managers XI in a testimonial match for Peter.

In a eulogy penned by Ernie Shepherd, the assistant manager at Roots Hall, Watson was described in these glowing terms: 'He will always be remembered for his tremendous efforts in all the games in which he played, he played in the true professional spirit, was fearless and shirked nothing, and was always prepared to run himself into the ground for the Blues.' The level to which he was admired as a player could be gauged by the people who made the journey to play for the Managers XI – Danny Blanchflower, Tommy Docherty, Bob Stokoe and Neil Franklin, to name but a few. He was only thirty-two at the time of his enforced retirement, but he took considerable pleasure in the rapid progress of his brother, who not only played in the same position, but also in a very similar style to Peter.

David Webb
Manager

Born: East Ham, London, 9/4/1946

Joined: June 1986, as manager

Other clubs: West Ham, 1962-63; Leyton Orient, 1963-66; Southampton, 1966-68; Chelsea, 1968-74; QPR, 1974-77; Leicester, 77-78; Derby County, 1978-80; Bournemouth, 1980-81; Torquay, 1984-85

David Webb was rejected by West Ham, but he made the grade at Leyton Orient, making his first-team debut in August 1964. He became a popular full-back, who often starred in a mediocre side. Webb went to Southampton in March 1966 and it was the Saints' manager, Ted Bates, who converted him to the centre-back role that would make his career. After two years at Southampton, Webb was sold to Chelsea where he was hero-worshipped for his fearsome tackling and upfield surges. Having won an FA Cup medal, a year later he added a European Cup Winner's Cup medal to his collection. During May 1974, he was transferred to QPR and later played for Leicester and Derby. It was surprising that he was never considered for international honours.

Webb joined Bournemouth as player-coach and, later, manager in 1980 and guided them to promotion in 1981/82. He left in 1983, taking many of his players with him, to join Torquay United. However, his side performed badly and Webb picked himself to play at Chester in November 1984. Webb scored the only goal in a 1-0 victory and played again the following January in the home game with Crewe. Webb departed from Torquay in the summer of 1986. He joined Southend and took over a dispirited squad from Bobby Moore, but within months had worked wonders, pushing the Blues into the promotion picture. In March 1987, Webb resigned following a bitter row with chairman Vic Jobson. However, his able deputy, Paul Clark, completed the task of gaining promotion to the Third Division.

By December 1988, his always-volatile relationship with Jobson had eased and Webb returned to Roots Hall, initially as general manager, with Clark remaining in charge of team affairs. However, Webb soon took over all duties and, despite suffering relegation in 1989, the future looked bright for the Blues. Webb galvanised a squad of journeymen and bargain-basement signings into a motivated and successful side, which gained unprecedented back-to-back promotions – Webb taking the club into the Second Division for the first time in its history. After a reasonably successful campaign in the higher echelon, Webb again quit the club following another row with Jobson. He moved to Brentford, where he became the club's owner/manager. His time at Griffin Park was forgettable, and Bees fans still hold him responsible for the disposal of some of their star players.

Webb resurfaced at Conference side Yeovil Town and, by October 2000, had turned them into a table-topping, fully professional outfit. He jumped at the chance of returning to Roots Hall for a third time, to replace Alan Little. For delighted Blues fans it meant the homecoming of the club's all-time most successful manager. However, after a year in charge, a health scare saw him stand down as manager.

Ronnie Whelan
Midfielder

Born: Dublin, 25/9/1961

Joined: September 1994, from Liverpool

First team debut: v. Stoke, 10/9/94

Appearances: 35

Goals: 0

Other clubs: Home Farm (Ireland), 1977-79; Liverpool, 1979-94

Ronnie Whelan's rise to legendary status began with Ireland club Home Farm. Ronnie Whelan first became associated with the club as a six-year-old, playing in the club's summer mini-leagues programme. By the age of nine he was already playing for the under-12 side. On his sixteenth birthday, the frail but talented midfielder made his full debut against Drogheda United in September 1977. He soon won schoolboy, youth and amateur caps for Ireland, before he was signed by Liverpool in 1979. In 1982, Bob Paisley described Whelan as the 'type of twenty-year-old footballer who stirs dreams in a sixty-two-year-old manager'. Whelan had made his Liverpool debut a year earlier, in April 1981, when he won rave reviews against Stoke. He scored after only 28 minutes, accepting a pass from Sammy Lee before running fifty yards and slotting the ball past Peter Fox in the Stoke goal.

Already an under-21 international, Whelan gained his first full cap later that year. Despite being only nineteen years old, Whelan was to remain an Anfield regular for the next thirteen seasons. Kenny Dalglish used to say that the first name on his team-sheet each week was that of Ronnie Whelan. By the time he left Anfield in 1994, Whelan's trophy cabinet consisted of a European Cup winners' medal, six League Championship medals, three League Cup winners' medals and an FA Cup winners' medal. He

also won the Young Player of the Year award in 1980 as well as 51 caps for his country. He played for Ireland in the World Cups of 1990 and 1994 and the European Championship of 1988.

He clocked up 506 appearances for Liverpool, scoring 70 goals in an illustrious career. He then played a single reserve game for Millwall, before joining Southend in September 1994. He fulfilled Peter Taylor's need for a quality midfielder to perfection. In truth, his deft skill and vision was often lost on his team-mates, but Southend fans were privileged to see such a gifted footballer wearing a Blues shirt. Despite his veteran status, his first season at the club saw him voted Player of the Year. He was then appointed as team manager but sadly in the first game of the 1995/96 season Whelan sustained a knee injury which was to end his playing career. His first season as manager saw the Blues finish in fourteenth place. His second campaign was a disaster, however, as Southend were relegated. Whelan's resignation was accepted by Vic Jobson.

Whelan resurfaced as coach of Greek First Division side Panionios for the 1998/99 season, when he guided them to the quarter-final of the last ever European Cup Winners Cup competition. However, in their domestic league his charges struggled and his contract was terminated. He subsequently took up a coaching post with Olympiakos Nicosia in Cyprus.

Arthur Williamson
Defender

Born: Ardblae, 26/7/1930

Joined: May 1955, from Clyde

First team debut: v. Leyton Orient, 3/9/55

Appearances: 287

Goals: 2

Other clubs: Clyde, 1950-55

Signed in May 1955 after spending four seasons with Clyde, Arthur holds a special place in the Southend United record books with a record which is unlikely ever to be beaten. A sturdy Scot – described in the Southend United handbook of 1961/62 as 'a strong tackler; quick in recovery' – he made his Blues debut at right-back in September 1955. After a run of 17 League and 2 FA Cup appearances, Dennis Howe displaced Arthur for two matches, but on his return to the right-back position on 7 January 1956, Arthur made the number two jersey his own. He played the remaining 20 League and 2 FA Cup matches during the 1955/56 campaign, and then was an ever present for the next four complete seasons. After playing in the Blues' famous 0-1 home defeat to Manchester City in the Roots Hall mud in the 1955/56 campaign, Arthur appeared in the 2-1 win over Liverpool and the 1-6 defeat to Birmingham City during the 1956/57 season, in which he opened his scoring account for the Blues with the only goal in a 1-1 draw at Vicarage Road against Watford.

The 1957/58 campaign saw two more matches in the FA Cup against Liverpool for Arthur, and also the arrival of his first milestone – his 100th consecutive match in the blue of Southend. This came on 28 December 1957 away to Queens Park Rangers, the game ending in a 1-1 draw. However, Arthur appeared to have no intention of breaking his run of consecutive appearances, and the 1958/59 season saw him ever-present in the number two jersey again, making 46 League and 2 FA Cup starts. During the 1959/60 campaign, Arthur notched up his 200th consecutive appearance, in the 1-3 defeat at The Dell against Southampton, but after 11 appearances in the 1960/61 season, Arthur lost his place to Pat Holton and the run ended on 230 consecutive League and cup games – his final appearance in the sequence being in the 0-2 home defeat to Swindon Town on 24 September 1960.

On his return to the first team on 10 December 1960, Arthur scored his second and last goal for the Blues in a 1-1 draw at Roots Hall against Grimsby Town, and he missed only two further matches that season. The 1961/62 campaign proved to be the last for Arthur at Roots Hall, as he was unable to displace Jimmy Shiels from his right-back berth, and he ended up making only 11 League and a solitary FA Cup appearance. Arthur was released by the Blues at the end of the 1961/62 season. He returned to his native Scotland and entered the butchery trade. Arthur's 269 League and 18 FA Cup appearances include those 230 consecutive appearances – a run that is unlikely to be even approached, let alone be beaten in these days of Bosman free transfers, contract wrangles and yellow and red card suspensions.

Steve Yates
Defender

Born: Burton-on-Trent, Staffordshire, 8/12/1953

Joined: November 1977, from Leicester

First team debut: v. Watford, 19/11/77

Appearances: 253(1)

Goals: 9

Other clubs: Leicester, 1971-77; Doncaster Rovers, 1983-85; Stockport County, 1985-86; Shepshed Charterhouse, 1986-88

Steve was a very successful sportsman whilst a student and could have become a star in any of the three sports he had an interest in. As a cricketer, Steve won England schools honours as a left-arm spinner and promising batsman and, as an athlete, he won the England schools discus title at the age of fourteen. However, it was football that Steve chose to follow as a career, being offered a chance by Leicester City, eventually turning professional in December 1971.

Steve played for Leicester City reserves for three years before making his first-team debut at the age of nineteen. However, being understudy to a player as consistent as Dennis Rofe meant very limited chances arose for first-team games, and eventually Leicester put Steve on the transfer list. In November 1977, after six years as a professional and only 19 first-team appearances, Steve joined the Blues. He made his Southend debut against Watford on 19 November 1977, the Blues winning 1-0. Yates went on to regularly fill the left-back position, his powerful displays bringing him many plaudits.

The 1978/79 season was another good one for Steve, who made 47 appearances, but 1979/80 proved to be not so good. He contracted food poisoning at a pre-season match and lost 13lbs in weight. He then crushed his ankle ligaments in October, and was out of action for nearly three months. To cap it all, the Blues ended the sea-son being relegated. If the 1979/80 campaign was forgettable for Steve, 1980/81 proved very memorable, as he missed only four matches as Southend stormed to the Fourth Division championship. In the next season, Steve racked up another 41 games.

After the 1982/83 season, in which the emergence of the young Glenn Pennyfather must have made Steve feel unsure about his future at Southend, he made only eleven starts, ten of which were at centre half, before the combination of Pennyfather and Steve Collins displaced him from the team. This proved too much for Steve, who wanted regular first-team football and, in December 1983, he travelled north to join Doncaster Rovers. Steve made 44 League appearances at Belle Vue, before brief loan spells at Darlington and Chesterfield, and a non-contract stay at Stockport County brought an end to his Football League career. He continued playing at non-League level by turning out for Shepshed Charterhouse.

Steve returned to Roots Hall in August 2000 to attend Ron Pountney's testimonial, although he was unable to participate in the veterans match due to injury. During his spell at Roots Hall, he kept his cricket skills finely tuned, playing for Southend in the Morrant Cricket League, and even turning out for the Essex Second XI on one occasion.